GREAT WESTERN
HALLS
& MODIFIED HALLS

GREAT WESTERN
HALLS
& MODIFIED HALLS

LAURENCE WATERS

PEN & SWORD
TRANSPORT

First published in Great Britain in 2015 by
Pen & Sword Transport
An imprint of Pen & Sword Books Ltd
47 Church Street
Barnsley
South Yorkshire
S70 2AS

ISBN 978 1 78383 145 6

Typeset by Pen & Sword Books Ltd
Printed and bound in China by Imago Publishing Limited

Typeset in Palatino

Pen & Sword Books Ltd incorporates the imprints of Pen & Sword
Archaeology, Atlas, Aviation, Battleground, Discovery, Family History,
History, Maritime, Military, Naval, Politics, Railways, Select, Social
History, Transport, True Crime, and Claymore Press, Frontline Books,
Leo Cooper, Praetorian Press, Remember When, Seaforth Publishing
and Wharncliffe.

For a complete list of Pen and Sword titles please contact
Pen and Sword Books Limited
47 Church Street, Barnsley, South Yorkshire, S70 2AS, England
E-mail: enquiries@pen-and-sword.co.uk
Website: www.pen-and-sword.co.uk

ACKNOWLEDGEMENTS

I would like to thank the following for their help in producing this book: Michael Berry, Steven Cooper, Anthony Doyle, Robin Isaac, Phillip Kelley, John Lewis, Peter Riley and Peter Speller.

Many thanks to the following photographers: A.E. Doyle, J.D. Edwards, the late Mike Mensing, Brian Morrison, the late Dr Geoff Smith, Bill Turner, and Derek Tuck. Also to Rodney Lissenden for the R.C. Riley images. Many of the photographs used are from the Great Western Trust Photo Archive at Didcot Railway Centre.

Ex-Oxford and Didcot enginemen, Gordon Goble, Jerry Coleman, Bob Cottrell, John Green, Alan Wills, and Alan Trego, have provided much additional information.

Individual locomotive details have been taken from the original Great Western locomotive record sheets that were collated together by the late Bill Peto, and are now held by the Great Western Trust at Didcot Railway Centre. I have also consulted original internal Swindon works documents relating to the naming of the *Hall* and *Modified Halls*.

I have also found the following publications to be very helpful: *Collett and Hawksworth Locomotives* by Brian Haresnape, the RCTS Railway Observer Magazines 1932-1966, the *Railway World*, *The Railway Magazine*, the *Great Western Magazine*, *The Locomotive, Railway, Carriage and Wagon Review*, and various Great Western, and Western Region operating timetables.

THE GREAT WESTERN HALL AND MODIFIED HALL CLASS 4-6-0s

The gradual growth of the railways in this country during the late nineteenth and early twentieth centuries in both passenger and, probably more importantly, freight traffic saw the requirement for a more powerful and more versatile type of motive power. All of the various companies probably faced the same problem, a need for steam locomotives that were equally capable of operating both passenger and freight services over much of their system. In other words, mixed traffic locomotives.

At the turn of the nineteenth century, Great Western passenger motive power comprised mainly 4-4-0 and 2-2-2 types designed by William Dean. The largest passenger engines at this time were the 4-4-0 *Atbara* class, producing a tractive effort of 16,010lbs. Good though these locomotives were, none were really powerful enough to haul the heaviest trains. As passenger numbers increased and trains became longer and heavier the Great Western was increasingly having to utilise double heading on many of its passenger services.

On 1 June 1902, George Jackson Churchward took over from Dean as the Chief Locomotive Carriage and Wagon Superintendent of the Great Western Railway. Churchward was born in Stoke Gabriel, Devon, in 1857. After an apprenticeship on the South Devon Railway, and when that railway amalgamated with the Great Western on 1 February 1876, he moved to Swindon, working his way up to Carriage and Wagon works manager, and in 1897 as the principal assistant to the Great Western's Locomotive Carriage and Wagon Superintendent, William Dean. Churchward took over the post of Locomotive, Carriage and Wagon Superintendant from Dean in 1902 and one of his first jobs was to produce a new range of more powerful passenger locomotives to help to alleviate this problem. His answer came in the form of two classes of 4-6-0 locomotives, the four cylinder *Star* Class, and the two cylinder *Saint* Class, both with

G.J. Churchward, Great Western Locomotive Superintendent 1902-1921.

6ft 8 1/2in driving wheels, and a standard Swindon no. 1 boiler, and his versatile 'go anywhere' 4300 class 2-6-0s. He also considered producing a medium-sized 2 cylinder 4-6-0 mixed traffic locomotive, again with a standard no.1 boiler but with 5ft 8in driving wheels, a design that would give a combination of good acceleration, and pulling power.

On any railway a good mixed

traffic locomotive is a vital factor in the running of both passenger and freight services and rather surprisingly Churchward failed to take this idea further. It was Collett that eventually used this design, when in 1936 he produced the very successful 2 cylinder 5ft 8in. driving wheel *Grange* Class 4-6-0s. Another important decision taken by Churchward was the introduction of standardised components into Great Western locomotive design, a decision that not only proved invaluable to the company over the years in terms of both construction and maintenance, but is of considerable benefit today, aiding massively in the preservation and restoration of former Great Western locomotives. Churchward's philosophy was to design and construct locomotives that were 'Horses for Courses' so to speak, in other words designed for specific use over the Great Western system. He took locomotive testing to a new level. Whilst still assistant to Dean, he was responsible for the construction in 1901 of the first modern Dynamometer Car, and also of the first stationary locomotive testing plant, which was opened at Swindon in 1903.

The 2 cylinder *Saints* were first introduced in 1906 and with a tractive effort at 85 per cent of 23,382lb, were considerably more powerful than the old 4-4-0s. The 4 cylinder *Stars* were introduced a year later, in 1907, and were even more powerful producing a tractive effort at 85 per cent of some 25,090lb. Churchward's 4-6-0s were very successful and formed the basis for future Great Western passenger and mixed traffic motive

C.B. Collett, Chief Mechanical Engineer 1922-1941.

power for the next fifty years. Such was the success of his designs, locomotives based on his original 4-6-0 concepts were still being built at Swindon by the newly formed Western Region right up until 1950.

Churchward retired in December 1921 and continued to live in Swindon. Even in retirement he regularly visited the works, and it was en route to one of these visits on 19 December 1933 that he was unfortunately hit and killed by the 08.55am Fishguard service whilst crossing the main line.

Churchward's successor, Charles Benjamin Collett, was born in London on 10 September 1871. The son of a journalist, his early experience was in marine engineering, working for Maudsley, Sons, and Field Ltd of Lambeth, expert marine engine builders. He joined the Great Western Railway in May 1893, working first in the drawing office and then progressing through the system at Swindon

becoming Works Manager in 1912, and Deputy Chief Mechanical Engineer in May 1919. Just as Churchward had been Dean's assistant, Collett became Churchward's assistant and took over from him as Chief Mechanical Engineer on 1 January 1922, Churchward having retired on 31 December 1921 (the title Locomotive, Carriage and Wagon Superintendent having been changed by the Great Western to Chief Mechanical Engineer in 1916). During his period in office Collett modernised workshop practice, and greatly improved locomotive manufacturing methods. This in turn increased the mileage between works overhauls. During the 1930s he greatly improved the locomotive testing plant at Swindon. He was also very safety orientated and extended the use of the Great Western Automatic train control system (ATC) to cover much of the Great Western main line. After his retirement he moved to Wimbledon and died on 5 April 1952 aged eighty-one.

Collett inherited a series of fine express passenger and mixed traffic locomotives, mainly comprising the *Saints*, *Stars* and the ubiquitous Churchward 4300 class 'Mogul' 2-6-0s. The heavy long distance goods services were in the hands of Churchward's 2800 class 2-8-0s, and suburban passenger services operated mainly by 2-6-2 tanks.

Collett's first priority was to replace some of the ageing passenger and mixed traffic classes with new locomotives. Collett obviously rated the *Stars* and the *Saints* highly, basing both his new *Castles* and *Halls* on these designs, and in doing so he

Saint Class 4-6-0 no. 2925 *Saint Martin*, pictured here in the early 1920s. Built at Swindon in September 1907 it was withdrawn from Shrewsbury on 6 August 1924 and taken to Swindon where it was converted into a prototype for the new *Hall* Class 4-6-0s. Notice the ATC apparatus fitted under the front buffer beam.

continued Churchward's standardisation policy.

In 1923 he produced the first of his 4 cylinder *Castle* Class 4-6-0s, a class that eventually numbered 171 locomotives, and became arguably the finest 4-6-0s in the country. The *Castles* were essentially an enlarged *Star*; in fact a number of *Stars* were eventually rebuilt as *Castles*. The new *Castle* Class locomotives were eventually used on all of the Great Western's crack trains. In 1927 he took the 4-6-0 design a step further with the introduction of the powerful 4 cylinder *King* Class 4-6-0s, which were used on the heaviest passenger services.

Around the same time that he was developing the *Castles*, the Great Western traffic department were asking for larger and more powerful mixed traffic locomotives. The Great Western had introduced express vacuum brake freight trains in around 1904, these services carried a variety of products, but often perishable commodities, such as milk, fish and meat, tended to be carried in vacuum braked vehicles that were attached to the rear of fast and semi-fast passenger services. Gradually, over time, the introduction of more vacuum braked wagons allowed many of these perishables to be carried, at the same speed as many passenger services, in fully fitted express freights, comprising individual fish, milk, meat, and vegetable trains, many of which travelled overnight

As already mentioned, by the 1920s many of the express fitted goods and secondary passenger services would have been in the hands of the 4300 class 2-6-0s. The small Moguls were introduced by Churchward in June 1911, and continued to be built by Collett right up until April 1932. The class eventually comprised 341 locomotives. Good as they were, they were generally acknowledged to be not great riders at speed, and

were probably a little short on power for the faster and heavier services. One option considered at the time was to rebuild the 4300s with a four wheel leading bogie and the larger no.1 boiler. This would have certainly given the 4300s more power, and would have hopefully improved their ride.

However, Collett chose not to go down this route, but instead he used Churchward's very successful 2 cylinder *Saints* as a basis for his new mixed traffic class Accordingly in December 1924 he took *Saint* Class no. 2925 *Saint Martin*, built at Swindon in October 1907, and replaced the 6ft 8in driving wheels with smaller 6ft diameter wheels. The only other major alteration made at this time was to fit a *Castle* design side windowed cab. Other than that no. 2925 was still essentially a *Saint* Class in regard to the boiler, cylinders, motion, frames, and front bogie. However, the new engine produced a tractive effort at 85% of some 27,275lb, somewhat more than the 24,395lb of the 1912 batch of *Saints*. The smaller driving wheels of the prototype also gave it better acceleration than the *Saints*.

Prior to modification no. 2925 had completed some 778,209 miles in service. It had been fitted with Automatic Train Control System (ATC) in the early 1920s. ATC had been introduced by the Great Western in 1906 on the Twyford to Henley and the Oxford to Fairford branches. In 1908 it was installed on the Great Western main line between Slough and Reading. The system was a great safety aid, and from March 1930 it was gradually extended over the whole system, and from the same date all new build locomotives were fitted with ATC.

There was talk at the time that a further nine *Saints* would be rebuilt with 6ft diameter wheels, but for whatever reason this did not materialise. Instead, and rather unusually, this single prototype ran essentially as a test locomotive between 6 January 1925, when it was allocated to Plymouth Laira, until 15 October 1928, when it entered Swindon Works for a Heavy Intermediate repair. During this extended test period it completed a total of 182,835 miles, and visited Swindon twice for Heavy

Intermediate repairs, first in January 1926 and again in August 1927.

During this period no. 2925 was allocated in turn to Plymouth Laira, Old Oak Common, Bristol Bath Road, and Penzance locomotive depots. Working from these depots allowed it to be assessed on a variety of services, both passenger and freight, and also working conditions. It allowed the locomotive department to gain valuable information on performance, coal consumption, and, of course, reliability, whilst also getting valuable feedback from the crews. The conversion proved to be a resounding success, and in December 1928 the first of a batch of 80 of the new 'Saint Martin' Class 4-6-0s were constructed at Swindon. I have used the term 'Saint Martin' Class as that is how they were described by Swindon at the time.

It is interesting to speculate if it was Collett's intention to withdraw no. 2925 once it had served its purpose, as the first of the class, *Adderley Hall*, initially carried the number 4900. However, this did not happen and no. 2925 was renumbered 4900 on 7 December

Pictured here at Swindon in December 1924 is no. 2925 *Saint Martin* after conversion into the prototype for the new *Hall* Class 4-6-0s. It is seen here in Swindon works photographic grey. It has been fitted with 6ft driving wheels and a *Castle* type cab with side windows, and is coupled to a Churchward 3,500 gallon tender no. 4054.

The first *Hall* to be properly constructed was no. 4901 *Adderley Hall* in December 1928. It is pictured here in Swindon works photographic grey and coupled to rebuilt Churchward 3,500 gallon tender no. 1649. It has not yet been fitted with ATC.

1928. Before it left the works *Adderley Hall* was numbered no. 4901. It would have been easy for Collett to have no. 4900 Saint Martin renamed as a *Hall*, after all the Great Western had an almost unlimited supply of potential *Hall* names, but for whatever reason this was not done, and 4900 became the only member of the *Hall* class not to be named after a *Hall*. In an internal works memo dated 2 May 1929 listing potential 'Hall' locomotive, names the new locomotives were still being referred to as the 'Saint Martin' Class. It is not until September 1930 that a further works memo listing another batch of new *Hall* names now refers to the 'Hall' class.

Apart from its name no. 4900 *Saint Martin* was always different from the rest of the *Halls* as the boiler and frames were set lower by 4 inches. At this time it was not fitted with outside steam pipes, but this was rectified in December 1948, when during a Heavy General (HG) repair at Swindon, it was fitted with non-standard short outside steam pipes, and a new front end, the shorter steam pipes being required for the lower pitched boiler. Even after these modifications it was still easily identifiable to the spotters of the time from other members of the Class, as it still carried its lower pitched boiler right through until

its withdrawal on 3 April 1959. I used to see it regularly, and it always appeared to be smaller than the rest of the class, particularly when attached to a rebuilt Churchward 3,500 gallon tender, as it was during its final years in service. In its fifty-two years of service as both a *Saint* and a *Hall*, 'Saint Martin' amassed a remarkable 2,092,500 miles. The principal dimensions of the rebuilt no. 2925 were: two 18 inch cylinders with a 30 inch stroke. The boiler had a tube heating surface of 1686.60sq ft and a firebox heating surface of 154.78sq ft, with a superheating surface of 262.62sq ft This gave a combined total heating

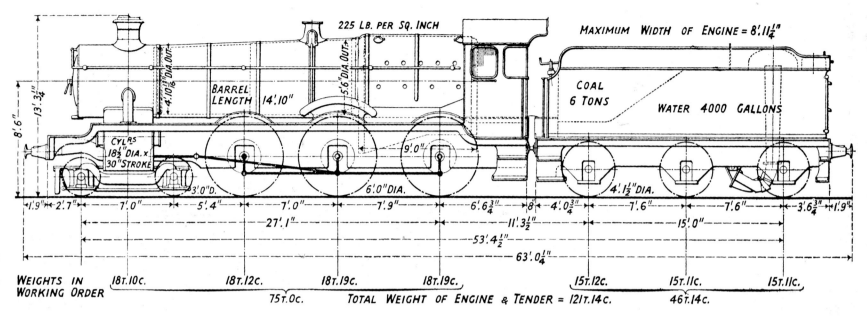

Diagram of 4900 Collett Hall.

surface of some 2104.00sq ft. The grate area measured 27.07sq ft with a boiler pressure of 225lb.

The first of the new *Halls*, no. 4901 *Adderley Hall*, was completed at Swindon in December 1928 and allocated from new to Penzance. In fact the the first fourteen members of the class were all initially allocated to the South West, being based at both Penzance and Laira, but as more were brought into service the class cascaded over the whole system. No. 4901 was the first of 259 Collett designed *Halls* that were constructed at Swindon between December 1928 and April 1943. They were followed by a further seventy-one Hawksworth designed *Modified Halls* that were constructed between March 1944 and November 1950. The new *Hall* Class differed from the prototype in that the no. 1 boiler centre was raised to 8ft 6in, the same as on the *Saints*, they were fitted with outside

steam pipes, smaller bogie wheels of 3ft diameter instead of 3ft 2in as on the *Saints*, and a modified frame. Other notable improvements saw the fitting of a new type of rocking shaft with the valve travel increased to 7 inches. The first batch, nos. 4901-4980 were also turned out with spring compensation beams for the driving wheels, but this was found to be unnecessary and the beams were removed as and when the locomotives passed through the works. The various modifications increased the engine weight by about 2 tons over the prototype. Other modifications took place over the next few years, ATC apparatus started to be fitted on new builds, commencing with *Hall* no. 4921 *Eaton Hall*, and apart from no. 4900, which already had it fitted, nos. 4901 to 4920 were all retrospectively fitted with ATC apparatus by 1930. Interestingly, between June 1934 and February 1935 nos. 5931

through to no. 5940 were fitted with apparatus for automatic clipping up of the ATC shoe. This was to enable working over electrified lines in the London area. In June 1931 and commencing with no. 5911 *Preston Hall*, all new *Collett Halls* were turned out with 9 inch piston valves as opposed to the 10 inch valves fitted to the earlier locomotives. The reduction in the diameter was achieved by fitting thicker valve liners inside the standard cylinders. From locomotive no. 5921 *Bingley Hall*, built in May 1933, all newly constructed locomotives were provided with a fire iron storage casing behind the rear splashers on the fireman's side. The feature proved to be popular with the loco crews, but was surprisingly not retrospectively fitted to any of the earlier locomotives. Also at this time the top mounted lamp bracket was moved from the top of the smokebox to a lower position on the front of the smokebox door. It is thought that no. 5922 *Caxton Hall* was the first *Hall* to receive this modification. During 1931-2 nos. 4941 *Llangedwyn Hall* and 4950 *Patshull Hall* were fitted with mechanical lubricators instead of the standard sight feed type. In 1947 no. 4905 *Barton Hall* was also fitted with mechanical lubrication. This was then applied from January 1950 to newly constructed Modified *Hall* nos. 7910-7929.

Collett's construction programme did not stop with the *Halls*, and in 1936 he introduced the first of his class of eighty 5ft 8in driving wheel *Grange Class* mixed traffic 4-6-0s. The introduction of these two classes gave the Great Western arguably some of the finest mixed traffic locomotives ever built in this country. Although the *Halls* were good, the *Granges* were generally acknowledged by the loco crews to be the best all round 4-6-0s on the Great Western. Such was the success of these two designs, other railway companies of the time used a similar formula for their own mixed traffic locomotives. On 1 January 1932 Collett's assistant, and Swindon Works Manager William Stanier was appointed Chief Mechanical Engineer of the London Midland & Scottish Railway. In 1934 he designed his own very successful 2 cylinder mixed traffic 'Class 5' 4-6-0s. With 6ft driving wheels, and an LMS design taper boiler, they produced a tractive effort of 25,455lb. Known as 'Black 5s', they proved to be exceptional locomotives, and were so successful that the class eventually numbered an astonishing 842 locomotives. In 1942 the LNER's Chief Mechanical

Engineer, Edward Thompson, produced his own two cylinder B1 class 4-6-0s, with 6ft 2in driving wheels, and a tractive effort of 26,880lb, they were yet another very successful mixed traffic design, of which 409 were built. Interestingly, after Nationalisation Robert Riddles used the 2 cylinder 4-6-0 layout, with 6ft 2in driving wheels, as the basis for his new Standard Class 5 mixed traffic locomotives.

The construction of the *Hall* class gave the Great Western a superb all round locomotive, and for thirty-six years they saw use on passenger and freight services over the Great Western, and later Western Region. With their route availability classified as D Red, the *Halls* were able to travel over much of the Great Western system, and their construction allowed the Great Western to withdraw many of the older 4-4-0 types. By 1934 all of the *Atbara*, *City*, *County*, and *Flower Class* 4-4-0s had passed into history.

Because of the need for mixed traffic locomotives *Halls* continued to be built at Swindon throughout the Second World War. Altogether some seventy-three *Collett Halls* were constructed between November 1939 and April 1943, and during this period they were turned out from Swindon without cabside windows, the first to have this modification was no. 5986 *Arbury Hall* which was completed on 21 November 1939. Existing members of the class had their cabside windows blanked off. Due to the austerity measures in place at the time, *Halls* nos. 6916 to 6958 that were built during this period were turned out without nameplates. Instead they had a small 'Hall

Class' painted on the centre splasher. After hostilities ceased the nameplates were gradually restored, and all had been refitted by 1948, the last being no. 6952 *Kimberley Hall* in August of the same year. Cabside windows were gradually replaced between 1945 and 1948.

The 6959 *Modified Halls*

On 5 July 1941 at the age of fifty-seven, Frederick William Hawksworth took over as Chief Mechanical Engineer from C.B. Collett who had retired at the age of seventy. Hawksworth was born in Swindon on 10 February 1884, his father was employed in the Swindon works drawing office, and his grandfather was the workshop foreman at Shrewsbury. Hawksworth had joined the GWR on 1 August 1898 as a 15-year-old works apprentice. Over the years he worked in a variety of posts at

F.W. Hawksworth, Chief Mechanical Engineer 1941-1949.

Swindon, ending up as Chief Draughtsman, having worked under both Churchward and Collett he obviously knew a thing or two about Great Western Locomotive design, and with his long service at Swindon was an ideal candidate for the post of Chief Mechanical Engineer. In many respects Hawksworth was unfortunate to take over at a time of wartime austerity. Wartime conditions meant that Swindon was under the control of the Mechanical Engineer's Committee of the Railway Executive, which meant that Hawksworth was unable to undertake any meaningful development work. With the railways running at maximum capacity at this time, and

locomotive reliability and servicing becoming an ever-increasing problem, there was a need for more mixed traffic types to help alleviate these problems. So one of his first tasks was to oversee the continued construction of the mixed traffic *Halls* and *Granges* for the Great Western, but also for the War Department, in the form of a large number of LMS designed class 8F 2-8-0s heavy freight locomotives, and it was not until 1944 that he was able to produce the first of his own designs.

Hawksworth had inherited a Great Western Railway Locomotive Department that was having to operate its services with an ever-decreasing quality of coal. To combat this problem he advocated

The first *Modified Hall* no. 6959 was turned out from Swindon in February 1944. It is pictured here brand new outside A shop on 29 February 1944. It is in wartime unlined black livery, and has no cabside window, or nameplates. The chimney is also painted black. It is coupled to Collett 4,000 gallon tender no. 4930, with the Hawksworth style coats of arms flanked by G.W. Its allocation code SWN (Swindon) is painted on the front frame, and a simple 'Hall Class' painted on the splasher in place of its nameplates. It was named *Peatling Hall* in December 1946. Notice above the cabside numberplate is a small white X; this indicates that normal loading can be exceeded on this locomotive.

using a higher degree of superheat on his locomotives, another of his decisions was to simplify and update the design and construction of his new 4-6-0 locomotives. This principle was applied to the *Modified Halls* in 1944, and the *County Class* 4-6-0s in 1945. The first of the new *Modified Hall* class locomotives no. 6959 was constructed at Swindon in March 1944, and the class became known

A low level shot of no. 6937 *Conyngham Hall* shows the improved ATC apparatus fitted within the front bogie frames of the later *Collett Halls* and also to all of the *Modified Halls* from new. The pickup was lighter and less bulky than the original ATC setup that was situated in front of the frames.

as the '6959' class. Due to wartime conditions, the first twelve *Modified Halls* nos. 6959 to 6970 were turned out without cabside windows, and also without nameplates. The cabside windows were gradually installed between 1945 and 1948, with the nameplates being fitted between 1946 and 1948.

To achieve the higher degree of superheat in the very successful Standard no. 1 boiler Hawksworth fitted a new three row superheater with a header regulator. These modifications gave an increased superheating surface over the two row superheated boilers from 263 to 314.6sq ft. To cope with this, nos. 6959-6965 were fitted with modified lubrication gear. Interestingly, the last five of the wartime built *Modified Halls* nos. 6966 to 6970, that were constructed between May and September 1944, were turned out from new with two row

superheaters, and these were also fitted with the modified lubricating gear. Construction of the locomotives was made simpler with the introduction of plate frames throughout. The new pattern cylinders were cast separately and then bolted to the plate frames that were extended through to the front buffer beam. A new fabricated smokebox saddle was also introduced. To make servicing easier, the Churchward bar frame bogie was replaced with a much simpler longer wheelbase version using plate frames, which were fitted with individual springs with the wheel diameter being reduced to 3ft. The modifications increased the wheel base of the *Modified Halls* over the *Collett Halls* from 7ft to 7ft 2in. They were all fitted with later type ATC apparatus with the pickup situated within the plate frame bogie. Other modifications

saw nos. 6959/60 and 6965/66/70, fitted with auto-feed drifting gear. This modification allowed a mixture of oil and steam to be fed to the valves and cylinders when the locomotive was 'drifting', and worked even when the regulator was fully shut. Other individual modifications saw no. 6965 *Thirlestaine Hall* fitted with a hopper grate, and no. 6967 *Willesley Hall* with a welded steel firebox. The higher degree of superheat worked wonders giving the 6959 class a much improved performance with the inferior coal of the time. In January 1950 mechanical lubricators were fitted as standard to the last twenty *Modified Halls*, commencing with no. 7910 *Hown Hall*. In October 1946 Hawksworth introduced a new design 4,000 gallon flush bottom straight sided tender of welded construction, and very similar to those that he had designed a year earlier for his new County Class 4-6-0s.

The new locomotives were fitted with 18in cylinders with a 30in stroke, exactly the same as the *Collett Halls*. The other principal dimensions were different and relate to the boiler which had a grate area of 27.07sq ft, and a larger superheating surface of 314.6sq ft. The tube heating surface was 1582.6sq ft and a firebox heating surface of 154.9sq ft, making a total combined heating surface of 2052.1sq ft. A later alteration made by Hawksworth saw the superheater elements shortened, thus reducing the superheating surface to 295sq ft; this had the effect of reducing the overall combined heating surface to 2032.95sq ft. The 27,275lb tractive

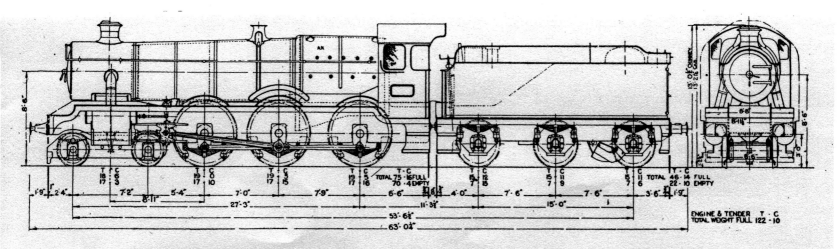

DESCRIPTION.

CYLINDERS (2):
Diameter .... 18⅛in.
Stroke .... 30in.
BOILER:
Barrel .... 14ft. 10in.
Diameter outside .... 4ft. 10¹³⁄₁₆in. & 5ft. 6in.
FIREBOX:
Outside .... 9ft. x 4ft. & 5ft. 9in.
Inside .... 8ft. 2⁷⁄₁₆in. x 3ft. 2⅜in. & 4ft. 9in.
Height .... 6ft. 6⅜in. & 5ft. 0⅜in.
TUBES:
Superheater .... No. 84, Diam. 1¼in., Length 14ft. 2in.
Fire ... No. 21, Diam. 5⅜in., No. 145, Diam. 2in., Length 15ft. 2⁷⁄₁₆in.

HEATING SURFACE
Superheater Tubes .... 314.60 sq. ft.
Fire Tubes .... 1,582.60 sq. ft.
Firebox .... 154.90 sq. ft.

Total .... 2,052.10 sq. ft.

AREA OF FIREGRATE .... 27.07 sq. ft.
WHEELS:
Bogie .... 3ft. 0in.
Coupled .... 6ft. 0in.
WATER CAPACITY, Tender .... 4,000 gals.
WORKING PRESSURE .... 225lb. per sq. in.
TRACTIVE EFFORT .... 27,275lb.
MINIMUM CURVE .... 8 chains normal, 7 chains slow

effort (at 85 per cent) was exactly the same as the *Collett Halls*, and placed the locomotives into the Great Western power classification D.

In 1919 the Great Western had introduced a system to show both the weight restriction, and power classification for each class of locomotive. As mentioned above under this system both the *Collett Halls* and *Modified Halls* were classified as D Red. D being for locomotives under 30,000lbs tractive effort, and Red for all locomotives over 17 tons 12cwt axle load. With their Red route classification the *Halls* were allowed to work over all of the Great Western main lines, and many of the secondary routes. The August 1938 edition of the

Great Western Railway Magazine provides a very comprehensive explanation of the GW system of classification, complete with diagrams etc. and also includes a list of all of the Great Western route restriction colour codes relating to both system mileage, and as a percentage of the system. On the list, Red classified locomotives are shown as being able to work over a total of 1,280 geographical miles, a figure which at that time represented 34 per cent of the Great Western system. Although the Western Region continued to use the old Great Western (D) power classification until the end of steam traction, British Railways designated all of the *Halls* and

Modified Halls as 5MT.

With their plate main frames, plate frame bogie, and straight sided tenders the *Modified Halls* had a much more purposeful and, dare I say it, a much more modern look than their Collett counterparts. They weighed slightly heavier at 75 tons 16cwt, with a further 46 tons 16cwt for the tender.

Interestingly the last *Modified Hall* to be built by the Great Western was no. 6980 *Llanrumney Hall*, which was completed at Swindon on 20 November 1947. The next in sequence should have been no. 6981 *Marbury Hall*, but this was not turned out from Swindon until 11 February 1948. Instead no. 6982 *Melmerby Hall* became the first to be

Diagram of 6959 *Modified Hall* Class.

Rather odd with its test equipment attached, no. 7916 *Mobberley Hall* stands in the yard at Swindon on 20 May 1951. It was in the works at this time for draughting tests.
Great Western Trust

built by British Railways; it was completed on 30 January 1948.

In the years after Nationalisation the railways in general had to cope with an increasingly variable quality of coal, which resulted in extra maintenance and poor timekeeping. On the Western Region tests were carried out at Swindon during 1951, using *Modified Hall* no. 7916 *Mobberley Hall*, to try and improve its performance, whilst using variable quality coal. Accordingly, between 18 January and 13 June 1951, no. 7916 was on loan to the Swindon Drawing office, and underwent numerous tests using the stationary test plant. Controlled road testing had been introduced by the Swindon Works chief test engineer, Sam Ell, in 1947. By using a steam flow meter in the cab, the driver could work the test locomotive at constant firing and steam production rates, over a set test route. Using the stationary test plant, other important information on both boiler and cylinder performance could be easily analysed. After some weeks of testing the Swindon team found that by removing the blastpipe jumper

ring, and modifying the dimensions of both the blastpipe and chimney, considerable improvements could be made to no. 7916's steaming rate. With the work undertaken proving a success, a number of *Modified Halls* also had their draughting improved and apart from the removal of the jumper ring, these locomotives were fitted with a narrower design of chimney, comprising straight sides and no capuchon. To signify those fitted with improved draughting a small 'ID' was stencilled on the front frame, behind the bufferbeam. The improvements were only made to the Hawksworth *Modified Hall* AK type boilers, but as time went on, and locomotives went through the works, some of these boilers were fitted to the earlier *Collett Halls*. The fitting of these boilers to the *Collett Halls* required a small modification to the outside steam pipes.

Nationalisation of the railways at the beginning of 1948 gave Hawksworth the distinction of being the last Chief Mechanical Engineer of the Great Western Railway, the post being abolished on Nationalisation, and he retired

just two years later on 31 December 1949. Although he also was responsible for the design of the 1500, 1600, and 9400 classes of 0-6-0PT shunting locomotives, he will probably always be associated with two types of Great Western 2 cylinder 4-6-0s, his very successful *Modified Halls*, and the perhaps less successful *Counties*.

One of his *Modified Halls* no. 6990 *Witherslack Hall* was one of three ex-Great Western locomotives selected by the Western Region to take part in the famous Locomotive Exchange trials, which took place between April and September 1948. The other two being a Collett 2800 class 2-8-0, and a *King* Class 4-6-0. The trials were held by the new British Railways Board who had appointed Robert Riddles as the new head of the new Electrical and Mechanical Engineers department. His task was to gather together different design and performance information from each of the big four companies that could be incorporated in the proposed new British Railways Standard designs. To do this a series of locomotive exchanges took place over a variety of routes using express passenger, mixed traffic, and heavy freight locomotives from each of the big four companies. Unfortunately, because of its restricted route availability no. 6990 *Witherslack Hall* could only be tested on services over the old Great Central route between Marylebone and Manchester. To achieve some continuity no. 6990 was worked by the same driver and fireman on each run. Unfortunately the *Modified Hall*'s performance was at best no more than average, and compared with other exchange

locomotives it showed up poorly in terms of coal consumption, actually coming second to last. This could have possibly been put down to using hard Yorkshire instead of soft Welsh coal during the test. Later tests using Welsh coal did actually reduce both coal and water consumption. It was left to the Churchward designed 2800 class 2-8-0 to 'fly the flag', so to speak, performing well in both fuel economy and performance. The Western Region also did their own testing, using another *Modified Hall*, no. 6961 *Stedham Hall*. The test train was operated between Bristol and Plymouth, but unlike no. 6990 this locomotive was fired using Welsh

coal, instead of the hard Yorkshire coal, and not unsurprisingly performed much better.

The oil burning experiment 1945-1950

In the years after the Second World War it would probably be true to say that Britain was essentially broke. The Government had to export as much as it could to bring in much needed foreign currency. To this end home consumption of manufactured goods went on the back burner. One plentiful commodity suitable for export was good quality coal, with some of the best being set aside 'for export

only', a policy that would have a profound effect on railway operations.

The decline in the quality of coal being supplied to the railways started to manifest itself soon after the start of war in 1939, and continued throughout the conflict. After the war had ended the situation did not improve and with the export drive starting to bite, the quality of coal being supplied to the railways remained poor. This was having quite an effect on both locomotive maintenance and timekeeping. The Great Western considered that one option to try and counteract this problem was to burn fuel oil instead of coal. In terms

In 1948, the almost new no. 6990 *Witherslack Hall* was chosen to take part in the inter regional locomotive exchanges that were held between April and September of the same year. Because of gauging problems, no. 6990 was confined to working services over the ex-Great Central lines between Marylebone and Manchester. It is pictured here on 15 June 1948 entering Marylebone on a service train. C G Stuart/Great Western Trust

In June 1946 *Hall* no. 5955 *Garth Hall* was converted at Swindon to burn fuel oil. The oil was held in a 1,950 gallon tank that was placed into the Churchward 3,500 gallon tender (no. 2141). The loco is seen here in ex-works conditionp; it was renumbered 3950 in October 1946. Notice it is fitted with a sliding shutter on the cabside window. This feature was fitted to all of the oil burning *Halls*. It was converted back to burn coal, regaining its original number 5955, in October 1948

of fuel efficiency oil had a much better calorific value over coal. So accordingly during the autumn of 1945 the Great Western, with the help of the Anglo Iranian Oil Company, started a programme to convert a number of 2800 class heavy freight locomotives to burn oil. The first locomotive to be converted was 2800 class 2-8-0 no. 2872 in October 1945, and this was followed by a further nineteen members of the class. Initially the 2-8-0s were put to work in South Wales hauling freight traffic between Llanelly and Severn Tunnel Junction,where refuelling facilities had been installed. The programme was extended when in June 1946 no. 5955 *Garth Hall* became the first passenger locomotive to be converted to burn fuel oil instead of coal. The conversion required an oil burner to be placed in the firebox grate area, with the fuel oil being stored in a 1,950 gallon tank that was situated in a Collett 3,500 gallon tender. Oil was fed by gravity to the burner where it was atomised by a steam jet incorporated in the burner.

Steam heating coils were installed to allow the oil to flow freely under adverse weather conditions, and a valve and connection were provided for lighting up the locomotive, with steam being taken either from another locomotive or from a steam line in the loco shed. After undergoing trials on local trains between Swindon and Gloucester, no. 5955 was used on main line services between Paddington and Bristol. The conversion to oil burning proved to be very successful, which resulted in the Government of the time getting 'in on the act' and sponsoring a large scale countrywide oil burning programme, that would eventually encompass all of the big four railway companies.

During 1947 the Great Western converted a further ten members of the Collett *Hall* class, but on these locomotives the 1,950 gallon oil tank was placed in the larger standard Collett 4,000 gallon type tenders. The fitting of the oil burning equipment altered the weight of the locomotive from 75 tons, to 75 tons

11cwt; however the weight of the tender increased substantially from 46 tons 14cwt, to 53 tons 3cwt. To identify those locomotives that were oil burners they were renumbered in the 3900 series. Interestingly no *Modified Halls*, or members of the *Grange* Class were converted. In October 1946 *Castle* class no. 5091 *Cleeve Abbey* became the first of five *Castles* to be converted to burn oil. Compared with coal, the oil burning locomotives were generally more efficient, and much cleaner to operate, with less work for the fireman, and of course there was no ash or clinker to dispose of. Right from the start the Great Western had taken the whole exercise seriously, and at some considerable cost had installed 36,000 gallon capacity oil storage tanks, and servicing facilities at a number of steam depots. At Old Oak Common a 350,000 gallon oil storage tank was installed. The Great Western initially intended to convert some eighty-five *Halls*, twenty-five *Castles*, seventy-three 2800 class 2-8-0s, and a single 4300 class 2-6-0. At this time the company was certainly considering the possibility of operating the bulk of the services in the South West using oil fired locomotives.

The problem was, of course, that the Government had given no real thought into the long term implications of using imported oil, and with financial austerity still in place, they soon realised that the country could not afford the cost of importing the oil. Subsequently the whole project including the Great Western's was scrapped. Perhaps right from the start someone should have considered the implications of exporting our best coal, whilst at the same time importing oil. Including the eleven *Halls* the Great Western had actually only converted thirty-seven locomotives comprising five *Castle* Class 4-6-0s, twenty 2800/2884 class 2-8-0s, and one solitary 4300 2-6-0 mogul (no. 6320) to burn oil. The whole exercise was a bit of a fiasco and was, in the end, a waste of money, particularly at a time when the country needed all of the money it could get. The Great Western lost a lot of money on the project, and by April 1950 all of the Great Western oil burners had been converted back to coal. Interestingly, the concrete and brick bases for the oil storage tanks that were installed at Didcot survived and can still be seen today.

The *Hall* Class oil burners were allocated as follows.

Nos. 3903 (4907), 3952 (6957), 3953 (6953), and 3954 (5986) to Old Oak Common

No. 3950 (5955) to Bristol Bath Road

Nos. 3900 (4968), and 3951 (5976) to Bristol St Phillip's Marsh

No. 3904 (4972) to Swindon

Nos. 3901(4971), 3902 (4948), and 3955 (6949), to Plymouth Laira

In a further experiment oil burner no. 3904 (4972 *Saint Brides Hall*), and *Hall* no. 5922 *Caxton Hall*, were equipped with experimental electric lighting during 1947 and 1949 respectively. Designed by the Metropolitan Vickers Electric Company Ltd the *Great Western Magazine* describes it thus: 'Current for the head and tail lamps, cab lighting and inspection lights is supplied by an alternator of rugged simple construction, using a permanent magnet for excitation.

The alternator is driven by an air turbine which is mounted on the right hand side of the smoke box. The air turbine is operated by means of a valve mounted on the steam fountain, the lights being selected via a series of switches in the cab.' For whatever reason, perhaps it was over complicated and unreliable, the experiment was discontinued, and the electric lighting was soon removed from both locomotives.

Tenders

The first twenty-three *Halls* were turned out from Swindon coupled

In May and June 1947 a further ten *Halls* were converted to burn oil. Pictured here speeding through the Thames Valley on a down parcels train is no. 3901 (4971) *Stanway Hall* from Oxley. It is coupled to Collett 4,000 gallon tender no. 2801. The whole oil burning experiment was unsuccessful and all eleven *Halls* were eventually converted back to burn coal. No. 3901 in April 1949.

to reconditioned Churchward 3,500 gallon tenders that dated from 1906, but had been strengthened with much stronger Collett designed frames. The Churchward tenders held 7 tons of coal and weighed in at 18 tons 5cwt empty, and 40 tons full. Some *Halls* also ran with Collett 3,500 gallon tenders nos. 2242-2268; these twenty-seven tenders were built at Swindon during 1929/30, they held 5 tons of coal and weighed in at 22 tons 5cwt empty, and 45 tons 3cwt full. One member of the class no. 4903 *Astley Hall* also ran for a short while during 1947, coupled to a rebuilt Dean 4,000 gallon tender no. 1459, that dated from 1900.

From locomotive no. 4961 *Pyrland Hall*, all successive *Halls* left the factory with the larger Collett 4000 gallon tenders. Some 481 of these tenders were built at Swindon between September 1926 and July 1946, and were used on a variety of Great Western classes. They carried 6 tons of coal, and weighed in at 22 tons 10cwt empty and 46 tons 14cwt full. The first batch of *Modified Hall* nos. 6959 to 6970, built between March and September 1944, were turned out from new coupled to these Collett 4,000 gallon tenders.

However in October 1947 and from no. 6971 *Athelhampton Hall*, all subsequent *Modified Halls* were turned out from Swindon with the new Hawksworth straight sided pattern tenders, no. 6971 being coupled to tender no. 4030. These new tenders were similar in design to the *County* Class tenders, and were of welded construction, but were 8ft wide (the *County* tenders measuring 8ft 6in). Numbered 4000-4126 they were used on both *Modified Halls* and *Castles*. The new tenders held 4,000 gallons of water and 6 tons of coal and weighed in at 23 tons, 5cwt empty and 47 tons, 6cwt full. Over time, many of these tenders were swapped around between the *Halls* and *Modified Halls*, which resulted in *Collett Halls* running with Hawksworth tenders, and *Modified Halls* with Collett tenders. A number of *Halls* also ran coupled to the unique Collett 8 wheel tender no. 2586. Built in August 1931, this tender weighed 24 tons, 19cwt empty and 49 tons, 8cwt full. It was coupled to no. 5904 *Kelham Hall*, with both tender and locomotive being withdrawn in November 1963. With the introduction of electrification on the West Coast main line, members of the Class that regularly worked 'under the wires', were coupled to Collett 4,000 gallon tenders that had been modified by fitting a large steel safety height bracket to the front of the tender. The brackets were known to the crews as 'goalposts'. The top held the 'overhead wires' warning sign, and made it slightly more difficult for the loco crews to climb up into the tender from the footplate. It also restricted the use of fire irons whilst under the wires. The modification was not needed on the Hawksworth 4,000 gallon tenders as the warning sign was attached to the large front bulkhead on these tenders.

Hall Class Names

The naming of Great Western passenger locomotives has always been an interesting topic for discussion, and was part of a tradition that stretched right back to broad gauge days. It was the Great Western publicity department, with input from the general public, that were generally responsible for finding suitable names for locomotives with, it seems, the final word often coming from the Chief Mechanical Engineer himself. In the early twentieth century Churchward had continued the naming policy with his *County* Class 4-4-0s, and his *Saint* and *Star* class 4-6-0s. The tradition was continued by Collett with the introduction of his *Castles*, *Granges*, *Kings*, *Halls*, and *Manors*, finishing with Hawksworth and his *County* class 4-6-0s.

The *Oxford English Dictionary* defines a 'Hall' as a Mansion, or large residence especially of a landed proprietor, or a University building set apart for residence or instruction of students.

The successful conversion of no. 2925 *Saint Martin* in 1924 saw the Great Western initially order eighty new *Hall* 4-6-0s. It is not clear at this time whether the Great Western was going to withdraw no. 2925 from service in 1928, or leave it to run on as no. 2925, as the first of the new class, *Adderley Hall*, initially passed through the works carrying the number 4900. However, an internal works memo dated 20 March 1928 states that its number should be altered to 4901 'to accommodate no. 2925 that is to be numbered 4900'. What is interesting is that even though the first eighty 'Hall' names had been allocated, this same works memo refers to the *Saint Martin Class*, as do further internal memos dated 17 October 1928, and 2 May 1929. However in a further memo dated 24 September 1930, instructing that 'the

Hall Class nameplates, top of page: no. 6960, middle: 4909, bottom: 6962.

name of no. 5900 should be altered from *Haddon Hall* to *Hinderton Hall*, the class is now referred to as the "Hall Class."' The name *Haddon Hall* was subsequently used on no. 5928. Incidentally no. 4900 *Saint Martin* is named after Martin of Tours born in 316AD, and who became Bishop of Tours in 371AD, and to whom many churches are dedicated.

One would have thought that with some 330 members of the *Hall* and *Modified Hall* class, finding names of *Halls* that were situated on the Great Western may have proved to be a difficult proposition. The late Bill Peto, who did extensive research into Great Western locomotive naming, found that there were at least four times as many stately homes with *Hall* names situated on the Great Western system than there were eventual members of the Class. So I wonder why the same criteria of only using names situated on the Great Western, that was applied to the *Castles*, was not applied to the Halls. (Collett had insisted that all of the *Castle* Class names should be on the Great Western system). It does appear that with the *Halls* a different approach was taken, with the whole country being scoured for suitable names, with quite a number being used that were not on the Great Western system at all. Perhaps as the *Halls* were designated as mixed traffic and not top link express locomotives Collett was not so involved. For example, one of the very first batch no. 4907 *Broughton Hall*, built in January 1929, is named after a building in Skipton, North Yorkshire. If you take some of the preserved *Halls* as further examples, no. 5900 *Hinderton Hall* is in the

Wirral Cheshire, no. 6960 *Raveningham Hall* is near Norwich, no. 6984 *Owsden Hall* is in Suffolk, no. 6990 *Witherslack Hall* is in Cumbria, no. 6998 *Burton Agnes Hall* is situated some 6 miles from Bridlington in East Yorkshire, and no. 7903 *Foremarke Hall* is near Derby; there were many other examples. Bill Peto came to the conclusion that the Great Western publicity department had probably used at least two reference books: *Country Seats* and *Baronial Halls*. Two Halls are thought to have never existed as buildings. *Toynbee Hall* (5961) is a community focused charity founded by Samual Barnett in 1884, and based in East London, and *Maindy Hall* (4942). Maindy is a an area in Cardiff, but may well have been a similar institution to Toynbee Hall.

Some of the Hall names related to Oxford University Halls of residence, and later Colleges: no. 4989 *Cherwell Hall*, is now part of St Hilda's College, no. 5914 *Ripon Hall*, is now a theological college, no. 5920 *Wycliffe Hall*, no. 5941 *Campion Hall*, no. 5947 *St Benet's Hall*, and no. 6909 *Frewin Hall* are actually buildings attached to some of the older Oxford Colleges. Other Halls such as no. 5960 *St Edmund Hall* (est. 1278), no.

7900 *St Peter's Hall* (est. 1929), and no. 7911 *Lady Margaret Hall*, have evolved over the years from Halls into actual Oxford colleges. Lady Margaret Hall founded in 1878 is particularly interesting, as it was the first academic hall for women in Oxford.

For such a large Class, alterations to the original lists of allocated names were few and far between. One early alteration saw the nameplates on no. 4985 corrected from *Allersley Hall* to *Allesley Hall*. It is well documented that Collett did not like apostrophes on the nameplates. However with many complaints from the public he eventually relented, and all apostrophes were eventually put on nameplates. For example, no. 5912 *Queens Hall* and no. 5947 *Saint Benets Hall* were altered to *Queen's Hall* and *Saint Benet's Hall*, respectively, on 9 April 1935.

Other alterations saw no. 5960 altered from *St Edmund Hall* to *Saint Edmund Hall* on 25 July 1935, and on 30 September 1949, the allocated name for no. 7921 *Salesbury Hall* was dropped and replaced by *Edstone Hall*. No. 7900, built in April 1949, was to be named *Coney Hall*, with the name *Saint Peter's Hall* allocated to no. 7920, but on construction they were swapped over, with no. 7900 becoming *Saint Peter's Hall* in April 1949, possibly to celebrate the twentieth anniversary of its founding in 1929, and no. 7920 being named *Coney Hall* in September 1950.

During the Second World War members of the class from nos. 6916 to 6958, which were built between June 1941 and April 1943, and *Modified Halls* nos. 6959 to 6970, which were built between March

1944 and September 1945, were turned out from new with cabside windows blanked out, and without nameplates, instead the inscription *Hall Class* being painted on the centre splashers. However, once hostilities had ceased the nameplates were gradually restored, and all had been fitted by 1948, the last one no. 6952 *Kimberley Hall*, built in February 1943, gaining its nameplates in September 1948.

In March 1962 an interesting name and number swap took place when no. 4983 *Albert Hall* was sent to Swindon for a Heavy Intermediate (HI) overhaul. In the works at the same time for withdrawal was no. 4965 *Rood Ashton Hall*. Whilst inspecting the two *Halls*, it was found that the frames of no. 4965 were in much better condition than those on 4983, and so were accordingly used to refurbish *Albert Hall*. As the name and number of a locomotive relate to the frames, the works should have turned out no. 4983 renumbered and named 4965 *Rood Ashton Hall*, but they did not, and subsequently no. 4983 left the works after its overhaul. Nothing was noticed at the time, and no. 4983 continued to run until its withdrawal from Old Oak Common on 28 December 1963. It was then sold as scrap to Woodham Bros, Barry who sold it on in October 1970 to The Birmingham Railway Museum at Tyseley. Subsequent restoration work discovered that the frames were in fact from the batch of *Halls* numbered 4901-4980, and after some detective work it was established no. 4983 should in fact be no. 4965 *Rood Ashton Hall*, and that is how it now runs. I wonder how many other *Halls* also had their

No. 4983 Albert Hall.

frames swapped by Swindon, we will never know. Towards the end of steam traction many of the *Halls* and *Modified Halls* as with other ex-Great Western 4-6-0s lost their nameplates and numberplates, and often both. Certainly by late 1964 shed foremen were directed by Swindon to remove nameplates as and when the locomotives came on shed, this of course was to avoid theft, as many had been sold, or allocated for sale. On some *Halls* the brass cabside numberplates were replaced with wooden replicas, no. 5971 definitely ran with a wooden replica cabside plate during the last months of its life.

Livery

When new, the *Collett Halls* were painted in GWR lined middle chrome green, with black cylinders and frames. This continued right up to the start of the Second World War, when, as they went through the works, mixed traffic locomotives were being turned out in unlined plain black livery. However, wartime conditions meant that with a general shortage of materials, maintenance schedules, and supplies of items such as paint were often disrupted, with the result that many locomotives went through the whole war period without being repainted. Also a shortage of loco shed staff at this time meant that cleaning went onto the back burner, resulting in many Great Western locomotives looking particularly scruffy. After hostilities ceased, and as they went through the works, many of the *Hall* class were again painted in Great Western lined green, with the Great Western coat of arms flanked by GW

The cabside of no. 5958 *Knolton Hall* showing the Red D Route availability and power classification, a white X indicating that normal loading could be exceeded and a white W, indicating a Western Region locomotive, a short lived scheme introduced in 1948, and only placed on a dozen or so *Halls*.

on the tender. The first *Modified Hall* to be painted in this livery was probably no. 6974 *Bryngwyn Hall*, when it was turned out new from Swindon in November 1947. Nationalisation brought a period of uncertainty to the railways with regard to liveries. In February 1948

no. 6983 *Otterington Hall* and no. 6984 *Owsden Hall* were both turned out from Swindon in Great Western lined green livery, with the number on the front bufferbeam, but with 'British Railways' lettering on the tender in Great Western style. Photographic evidence shows that this livery was also applied to nos. 6985/6986/6987/6988/6989 and 6990 *Witherslack Hall*. It is thought that no. 6990 *Witherslack Hall* was the last modified *Hall* to receive this livery. However, this livery was not adopted, as the newly formed British Railways Board brought yet another change of livery for the *Halls*, with the class being painted in the new British Railways corporate mixed

Once the new mixed traffic lined black livery had been decided, it was applied to Old Oak Common Hall no. 6910 *Gossington Hall*, seen here passing Westbourne Park on 29 July 1948. The loco had been on display at Paddington to show the new livery to the press and the public. The newly introduced lion and wheel crest can be seen on the tender. The locomotive was also fitted with a brass smokebox numberplate. Also on display at Paddington on the same day were *Castle* no. 5023 *Brecon Castle* in apple green livery, and *King* no. 6009 *King Charles II* in ultramarine blue. C G Stuart/ Great Western Trust

traffic lined black, with the newly introduced BR lion and wheel emblem on the tender. During this transition period a number of *Halls* and *Modified Halls* including no. 6983 received a small W painted under the cabside numberplate, to denote Western Region, but this was soon abandoned. Certainly until the introduction of the new lion and wheel emblem in June 1948, locomotives were still being turned out from Swindon with the words 'British Railways', again in Great Western style block capitals painted on the tender, and apparently due to a shortage of the new lion and wheel stencils, some were turned out without any inscription at all.

The first *Hall* to be painted in the new mixed traffic black livery was no. 6910 *Gossington Hall*, whilst in Swindon for a Heavy General (HG) repair June 1948; the new livery was displayed to the public when the locomotive was exhibited at Paddington on 29 July 1948, together with Castle no. 5023 *Brecon Castle* in apple green livery, and *King* no. 6009 in ultramarine blue livery, neither of which were subsequently adopted. At this time no. 6910 was also fitted with a brass smokebox numberplate, which it carried until its withdrawal in October 1965. Fellow class member no. 5954 *Faendre Hall* was also fitted with a brass front numberplate. During 1950 a number of *Halls* were turned out from Swindon with red backgrounds to their cabside numbers and nameplates, but this practice was not continued. One reason given was that the red paint faded quickly, another I have heard was that the cabside numbers were more difficult to see with red backgrounds.

The first new *Hall* to be fitted with a cast iron smokebox numberplate was no. 6991 *Acton Burnell Hall* in November 1948, oval smokebox shed identification plates were fitted to Western Region locomotives from about February 1950 and by 1951 most of the *Halls* had received both.

The mixed traffic lined black livery was abandoned by the Western Region during 1955 when Swindon started to turn out many classes in fully lined middle chrome green passenger livery, which also included its black mixed traffic Class 4-6-0s, initially still with the BR lion and wheel emblem on the tender. The first *Hall* to be turned out in the new livery is thought to have been no. 6997 *Bryn-Ivor Hall* in October 1955, whilst in Swindon for a heavy general (HG) repair. However from March 1957 a new crest comprising a red lion atop a crown, encircled and flanked by 'British Railways' was introduced by BR, and from that date all ex-Great Western passenger and mixed traffic locomotives passing through the works were turned out with this crest on the tender. Oxford allocated no. 7900 *St Peter's Hall* ran for a short time in the early 1960s with a red backed smokebox numberplate, the unofficial livery, being applied by a member of the shed staff.

At work

When new, the first fourteen *Halls* were allocated to the West Country, notably Penzance and Laira, here they took over many of the main line services in the South West from the Churchward *Bulldog* 4-4-0s, and also the 4300 *Mogul* 2-6-0s. The *Halls* proved to be excellent performers over the undulating gradients between Plymouth and Penzance, and with the weight allowance for a *Hall* on these services being set at 385 tons, they could manage most of them completely unassisted. Gradually, and as more and more were built, and with their Red route availability, the *Halls* cascaded over much of the Great Western system, with many of the main locomotive depots gaining examples of the class. They were soon to be seen working on both passenger and freight services in West Wales, the Midlands, the North West, and of course the Home Counties. Right from the start the *Halls* proved to be fine performers: in 1932 the *Railway Observer* reported that sharply timed trains, such as the 9.53am service from Newbury to Paddington (55.1 miles in 57 min), and the 1.45pm Newbury to Lavington (33.8 miles in 36 min) are almost invariably hauled by members of the *Hall* class that are in the Weymouth link. Another report states that the 9.53 ex-Newbury service, hauled by no. 4953 *Pitchford Hall* with nine 'eights', less one slipped at Reading, made the 53-mile run to Paddington, including a signal check at Royal Oak in 54 mins 44 sec. Again in January 1932 the *Railway Observer* reported that no. 4950 *Patshull Hall* with 358 tons tare on the 6.00pm service from Birmingham to Leamington was credited with attaining a maximum speed of 85.7mph on Hatton Bank, making the Leamington stop in even time. In October 1933 no. 4960 *Pyle Hall* from Oxford shed was reported as leaving Paddington with the 09.50pm service to

Plymouth and Penzance comprising sixteen coaches including four sleeping cars.

Halls had started to be used on inter-regional excursions from the early 1930s, travelling through to both Bournemouth and Portsmouth. They also began to see regular use on services from the West Midlands to the South Coast and also from Cardiff and Bristol to Portsmouth Harbour. Locomotives used on the Portsmouth services being turned and serviced at the LSWR shed at Fratton. Another regular service to use *Halls* was the Cardiff to Bristol, and Bristol to Salisbury services. Initially servicing took place at the Great Western shed at Salisbury, but after this shed was closed. In November 1950, they used the nearby ex-LSWR shed.

From the mid-1930s *Halls* were regularly used on many of the cross country services from the South Coast to the East Midlands and the North East, via Banbury, and over the old Great Central to Rugby and beyond. The *Railway Observer* reported an interesting working that took place on Sunday, 22 April 1934 when no. 4963 *Rignall Hall* from Reading broke new ground, being noted passing through Nottingham Arkright Station en route to Nottingham Victoria with an excursion from the south consisting thirteen Southern Railway coaches. This may have been the first time that a *Hall* had travelled so far north over ex-Great Central metals. During the war the 10.10am service from Southampton to Newcastle, known at this time as the 'Furlough', as it was used by troops going on leave, was regularly hauled by a Great Western

locomotive, often a *Hall*, through to Woodford Halse. After the war the service ran from Bournemouth once again being hauled by a Great Western locomotive, usually a *Hall*, between Basingstoke and Woodford Halse. By the 1950s *Halls* were being used on a regular basis on the Newcastle to Bournemouth West service running between Oxford and Basingstoke, occasionally running right through to Bournemouth. They were also noted running northwards over the old Great Central route via Banbury through to Rugby and Leicester. Great Western locomotives that operated these services to Leicester were serviced at Leicester GC shed, until it was closed on 6 July 1964, after which *Halls* often worked through to Nottingham. These services were a regular Banbury or Oxford turn, but Swindon crews were also passed to work through to Leicester. On 12 March 1964 no. 7912 *Little Linford Hall* from Banbury excelled itself by travelling right through to Sheffield Victoria whilst working the 10.50am Bournemouth to York service. The *Modified Halls* in particular saw considerable use on Class 1 passenger services. For example, during the 1950s and 1960s on summer Saturdays, the 'Royal Duchy' service between Paddington and Penzance became a regular *Modified Hall* turn.

There is no doubt that the *Halls* were held in high regard by the drivers and firemen that worked on them. Over the years I have spoken to many ex-Oxford drivers and firemen, and they all loved the *Halls*, particularly the *Modified Halls*. I must add that they liked the

Granges even more! Oxford had gained its first allocation of *Halls* in 1931, and thereafter had a steady allocation of fourteen or so Collett examples right up until the end of steam traction in 1965. It was the three long-serving *Modified Halls*, no. 6970 *Haddon Hall*, 7900 *Saint Peter's Hall*, and 7911 *Lady Margaret Hall*, that were many of the Oxford loco crews favourites. Although used on freight and parcels trains, they saw considerable use at Oxford on class one passenger trains, to Worcester, Paddington and also the fast cross country services to and from the South West to the West Midlands, and the North East. Many of the locomotive crews rated a good *Modified Hall* to be on many occasions, as good as a *Castle*. The fastest train of the day from Oxford was the 5.35pm non-stop service to Paddington. Its 60 minute schedule was well within a *Modified Hall*'s capabilities. This service was usually operated by an Oxford crew, using a Worcester or Old Oak based *Modified Hall* or a *Castle*, but occasionally an Oxford based *Modified Hall*. The 5.35pm service generally had a loading of just six coaches and it was well known locally that many of the Oxford drivers would 'have a go'. This resulted in a number of excellent times being recorded using a *Modified Hall*. On one such occasion Old Oak Common based no. 6974 *Brygnwyn Hall* completed the 63 miles in just 55min 30 seconds, and on another occasion no. 7904 *Fountains Hall* again from Old Oak, took just 55 min 39 sec.

Even in their final days the *Halls* were still capable of excellent running, as was demonstrated on 9

WESTBURY to TAUNTON
"The Great Western" Special
Saturday 9th May 1964

Timed by J R Moore
and D W Tuck

6999 "Capel Dewi Hall"   7 Coaches 243 tons tare 265 tons gross
Driver A Perfect   Firemen D Godden & B Green
Inspector Andress (Old Oak Common)

Dist		Mins	Secs	Speed
00.00	WESTBURY	00	00	
01.45	Fairwood Junction Box	02	55	45
04.70	Clink Road Junction Box	06	58	56½
06.75	Blatchbridge Junction Box	08	57	65
10.85	Witham	12	50	61½
12.70	Brewham Box	14	40	55½
16.15	Bruton	17	54	71
19.60	Castle Cary	20	53	62*
21.70	Alford Halt	22	46	72/76
24.50	Keinton Mandeville	25	00	74
26.65	Charlton Mackrell	26	46	76/82
30.00	Somerton	29	19	79½
32.15	Long Sutton & Pitney	31	00	82
34.20	Langport East	32	27	85
35.25	Curry Rival Junction Box	33	11	86½
39.20	Athelney	36	05	79
42.45	Cogload Junction	38	35	77
44.75	Creech Road Junction Box	40	24	77
47.20	TAUNTON	43	14	

Timing chart of 6999's run from Westbury to Taunton on 9 May 1964.

May 1964 when *Modified Hall* no. 6999 *Capel Dewi Hall* had its moment of glory. The Western Region ran a high speed special from Paddington to Plymouth to celebrate no. 3440 *City of Truro*'s 100mph run in 1904. Castle no. 4079 *Pendennis Castle* was booked to take the train to Plymouth but having achieved 96mph near Lavington it failed with collapsed firebars. It was removed from the train at Westbury where no. 6999 *Capel Dewi Hall* was the only spare locomotive capable of hauling the high speed special onwards. No. 6999 was actually in quite good condition having left Swindon works on 24 October 1963 after a Heavy Intermediate (HI) repair.

The 47.2 miles from Westbury to Taunton were reeled off in just 43 min 14 sec, a start to stop average of

65mph with a maximum speed of 86mph on the short descent from Somerton Tunnel to Curry Rivel Junction. Over the 20-mile section between Keinton Mandeville and Creech Junction the speed did not drop below 75mph. Ex-Western Region driver Ted Abear remembers talking to Brian Green who was one of the fireman on 11 June, who recalled that 'old Alf Perfect, the driver was in tears at Westbury after the failure of 4079. On arriving at Westbury they were given *Modified Hall* no. 6999, and off they set, and once they had got the fire right, it soon became clear that no. 6999 was a goer, and he and Dave Godden the other fireman got stuck into her, and she romped away with the train.' Alf and Bill Andress (the Old Oak Common Loco inspector) saw how she was running and decided to let Taunton know that they did not want to change engines by throwing a note out at Castle Cary, asking to let them run on to Plymouth so that they could get some time back'. Brian Green also relates that 'Alf was spitting feathers at Taunton about being stopped, and having to change engines.' No. 6999 lasted until the end of Western Region steam, being withdrawn from Oxford on 31 December 1965.

Allocations

The *Halls* were spread over the whole system, and it is interesting to note just how far flung some were. In 1947 there were twenty *Halls* and *Modified Halls* allocated to West Wales depots, of which three were as far West as Fishguard

(Goodwick), situated 287 miles from Paddington. These three *Halls*, nos. 5905 *Knowsley Hall*, 5908 *Moreton Hall*, and 5928 *Haddon Hall* are worth mentioning as they were allocated to Goodwick for many years. No. 5905 from 24 August 1933 until its withdrawal on 29 July 1963, no. 5908 from 12 January 1933, until 17 January 1962, and no. 5928 for the whole of its working life from 21 June 1933 until its withdrawal on 11 May 1962. All three would have been rare sightings in London. Legend has it that written in pencil on a signal post at the end of Paddington Station was the inscription: 'In loving memory of John Smith who died here whilst waiting for no. 5928 *Haddon Hall*.'

There were twenty-five in the West of England with six examples working from Penzance some 326 miles from Paddington. The Wolverhampton Division had seventy-four of which six were allocated to Chester some 214 miles from Paddington (via Oxford).

My local steam depot Oxford (81F) was always a *Hall* and *Modified Hall* stronghold, and saw many different examples allocated there over the years. Oxford gained its first *Hall*, the unfortunate no. 4911 *Bowden Hall*, on 19 September 1931, and between that date and its closure to steam on 31 December 1965, some ninety-one different members of the class comprising sixty-four *Collett* and twenty-seven *Modified Halls* were officially allocated to Oxford. The longest serving *Hall* was no. 4921 *Eaton Hall*. It arrived at Oxford from Old Oak Common in August 1932, and remained at Oxford until it was allocated back to Old Oak Common, some twenty-seven years later on 9 December 1959.

It is also worth noting that three *Collett Halls*, and five *Modified Halls* spent the whole of their working life at one depot. As already mentioned, no. 5928 *Haddon Hall* at Goodwick (87J), no. 5951 *Clyffe Hall* at Gloucester (85B), and no. 6954 *Lotherton Hall* at Bristol Bath Road (82A). There were five BR built *Modified Halls* nos. 7902 *Eaton Mascot Hall* and 7903 *Foremarke Hall* at Old Oak Common (81A), no. 7918 *Rhose Wood Hall* at Tyseley (84E), no. 7919 *Runter Hall* at Reading (81D), and no. 7928 *Wolf Hall* at Worcester (85A).

As already mentioned the *Halls* were distributed over much of the Great Western system. In 1947:
Paddington division 66
Bristol division 47
Newton Abbot division 25
Wolverhampton division 74
Worcester division 23
Newport division 25
Neath division 20
Total 280

In 1954, Western Region
Paddington (81) division 83
Bristol (82) division 56
Newton Abbot (83) division 48
Wolverhampton (84) division 55
Worcester (85) division 31
Newport (86) division 35
Neath (87) division 21
Total 329

The regional boundary changes of the early 1960s saw a number of *Halls* transferred to London Midland Region book stock, for clarity I have grouped those in the original Western Region divisions. In 1964 they were distributed-

Paddington (81) division 53
Bristol (82) division 27
Newton Abbot (83) division 17
Wolverhampton (LMR 2) division 37
Worcester (85) division 19
Newport (86) division 36
Neath (87) division 8
Total 197

Withdrawals

The first member of the class to be withdrawn was Truro allocated no. 4911 *Bowden Hall*, this was partially destroyed at Keyham during a German air raid on Plymouth on 29 April 1941. The remains of the badly damaged locomotive were taken to Swindon on 22 May 1941, where they were officially condemned. The prototype no. 4900 *St Martin*, having completed well over 2 million miles in service was the next to be withdrawn on 3 April 1959, quickly followed by Taunton based no. 4940 *Ludford Hall* on 9 November of the same year. Only two members of the class were withdrawn in 1960, no. 5915 *Trentham Hall* from Swindon on 13 January 1960, and no. 4901 *Adderley Hall* from Oxley on 16 September. A further eight were withdrawn in 1961. It was not until 1962 that heavy withdrawals of the *Collett Halls* took place with seventy-three examples being condemned, a further fifty-six went in 1963, with a further sixty-seven being withdrawn during 1964, leaving just forty-four examples running into 1965. Nine of which, nos. 4920, 5971, 6923, 6932, 6937, 6951, 6952, 6953 and 6956 lasted to the end of steam traction on the Western Region, all being withdrawn in

December 1965. The oldest survivor is the now preserved no. 4920 *Dumbleton Hall*. It was built at Swindon in March 1929, and was withdrawn from Bristol Barrow Rd on 10 December 1965, but ended up in store at Oxford. Another preserved *Hall*, no. 4936 *Kinlet Hall*, was built at Swindon just three months later in June 1939, but did not last quite so long in service, being withdrawn from Cardiff East Dock on 15 January 1964.

The first *Modified Hall* to be withdrawn was no. 6962 *Soughton Hall* from Old Oak Common on 7 January 1963. The shortest surviving member of the *Modified Hall* class was no. 7921 *Edstone Hall*, completed at Swindon on 8 September 1950. It was withdrawn after just thirteen years and 482,155 miles in service on 16 December 1963. It had spent much of its working life at Chester and Shrewsbury, finishing its days in service at Old Oak Common. A number of *Modified Halls* also lasted right up until the end of steam traction on the Western Region. As mentioned above, the first *Modified Hall* was withdrawn in January 1963, and this was followed by a further five other members of the class during the same year. A further twenty-two were withdrawn in 1964, and the final forty-three during 1965. With steam working on the Western Region drawing to a close, Oxford became the last bastion of the *Halls*, and *Modified Halls* on the region. Both the shed and yard area became a dumping ground for withdrawn members of the class. A few of the *Halls* and *Modified Halls* continued working right up until the 31

Oxford MPD became the last dumping ground for withdrawn *Halls* and *Modified Halls* en route to the scrap yards of South Wales, and the West Midlands. Pictured here in early January 1966 are at least a dozen of the thirty plus withdrawn *Halls*, *Modified Halls* and *Granges*, that were stored here at this time.
Great Western Trust

December 1965, the end of steam traction on the Western Region. Nos. 6956 *Mottram Hall*, 6991 *Acton Burnell Hall*, 6998 *Burton Agnes Hall*, and 6999 *Capel Dewi Hall* were all still working in the Oxford area during the final week. No. 6999 *Capel Dewi Hall* was on station pilot duty at Oxford on the very last day. However, on Saturday, 1 January 1966, Didcot driver Bob Cottrell remembers working the Banbury to Basingstoke perishables, from Oxford through to Basingstoke hauled by *Modified Hall* no. 7924 *Thorneycroft Hall*. At Basingstoke the *Hall* came off and was turned on the

shed turntable, prior to working back light engine to Oxford, where Bob tells me he then took the loco on shed, and placed it on the scrap line still with its fire intact, and in steam. The last example to work a scheduled passenger service on the Western Region was no. 6998 *Burton Agnes Hall*, built in January 1949, it hauled the 2.10pm cross country service from Bournemouth to York between Oxford and Banbury on 3 January 1966. This was the last official Western Region steam working. The engine had been officially withdrawn on 31 December 1965, but was specially

steamed for the occasion. The *Hall* was spruced up, and Oxford boilersmith Len Cross made a pair of replica wooden nameplates for its final run to Banbury. For the occasion the Lord Mayor of Oxford Alderman Mrs Kathleen Lower joined Driver Tony Faulkener and fireman Pat Cook on the footplate for the short trip from the shed to the station. No. 6998 was sold in running order to the Great Western Society during the following week.

On 26 December 1965 the following were noted at Oxford as stored out of use, Collett *Hall* nos. 4920, 4962, 6910, 6921, 6927, 6931,

6932, 6944, 6947, 6957, and *Modified Hall* nos. 6967, 6969, 6984, 6990, 6993, 7904, 7907, 7909, 7914 and 7927.

In terms of mileage the lowest was surprisingly not no. 4911 *Bowden Hall* – this locomotive actually ran a total of 558,921 in service before it was destroyed in the air raid – but was probably no. 7927 *Willington Hall*, completed at Swindon on 24 October 1950, and allocated to Reading, Old Oak Common and Cardiff Canton before being withdrawn from Oxford on 31 December 1965. When mileage recording stopped on 28 December 1963 it had run just 456,347 miles in its short working life. The highest mileage recorded for a *Hall* class proper was probably attained by no. 4927 *Farnborough Hall*, completed at Swindon on 21 May 1929. Records show that it completed a total 1,416,636 miles in service, prior to being withdrawn from Llanelly on 23 September 1963. Apart from no. 4911, records show that all of the first 100 members of the class attained a million miles or more in service.

In conclusion, they say that history often repeats itself, and that is exactly what is happening at Didcot Railway Centre, where the Great Western Society are currently converting no. 4942 *Maindy Hall*, built in July 1929, into a *Saint Class 4-6-0*.

Of the 330 *Halls* and *Modified Halls* built, eleven *Collett Halls*, and seven *Modified Halls* have made it into preservation. Apart from no. 4942 mentioned above, the frames and other parts of *Modified Hall* no. 7927 *Willington Hall* are being used

to reconstruct a Hawksworth 4-6-0 *County*, again at Didcot Railway Centre, with the boiler being used for the 6880 *Betton Grange* project at Llangollen. All of the others are either undergoing restoration, or have been restored to running order. Locations given are at the time of writing

No. 4920 *Dumbleton Hall*, Dart Valley Railway
No. 4930 *Hagley Hall*, Severn Valley Railway.
No. 4936 *Kinlet Hall*, Gloucester and Warwickshire Railway
No. 4942 *Maindy Hall*, Didcot Railway Centre, under conversion to Churchward Saint Class 4-6-0.
No. 4953 *Pitchford Hall*, Epping and Ongar Railway.
No. 4965 *Rood Ashton Hall*, Tyseley.
No. 4979 *Wootton Hall*, Ribble Railway, Preston.
No. 5900 *Hinderton Hall*, Didcot Railway Centre
No. 5952 *Cogan Hall*, Llangollen (some parts being used for Grange project)
No. 5967 *Bickmarsh Hall*, Northampton Steam Railway
No. 5972 *Olton Hall*, West Coast Trains based at Carnforth

Modified Halls
6960 *Raveningham Hall*, West Somerset Railway.
6984 *Owsden Hall*, Swindon and Cricklade Railway
6989 *Wightwick Hall*, Quainton Road
6990 *Witherslack Hall*, Great Central Railway Loughborough
6998 *Burton Agnes Hall*, Didcot Railway Centre
7903 *Foremarke Hall*, Gloucester

and Warwickshire Railway
7927 *Willington Hall*, Didcot Railway Centre, being rebuilt as a Hawksworth County Class 4-6-0, boiler being used for 6880 Betton Grange project.

Western Region Shed Codes used in book

In 1918 the Great Western introduced seven regional divisions with locomotives being allocated shed codes to indicate their allocation to depots within that division. From around 1922 the initials (shed code) of the locomotive's home shed were stencilled inside the cab, and later on the front end of the main frames, for example Old Oak Common was (PDN), and Bristol Bath Road (BL).

After Nationalisation, a new system of numerical shed codes was introduced, with the new Western Region being divided into nine loco divisions, ranging from eighty-one (London Division), through to eighty-nine (Oswestry division). The new locomotive shed codes were displayed on an oval cast iron plate, attached to the lower front of the smokebox door. As already mentioned with their Red route classification, the *Halls* and *Modified Halls* worked over much of the system, and it is no surprise that examples were at various times allocated to loco sheds in eight of those divisions.

The following shed codes have been used in both the main text, and photo legends.
81A Old Oak Common
81C Southall
81D Reading

On 7 December 1928 no. 2925 was renumbered no. 4900. It is pictured here coupled to rebuild Churchward 3,500 gallon tender no. 1934 inside the shed at Reading around 1930. The shed was being rebuilt at this time from a round house into a straight shed, with the partially disused 65ft turntable, which was removed in 1931, in the foreground. Great Western Trust

81E Didcot
81F Oxford
82A Bristol Bath Road
82B Bristol St Phillips Marsh
82C Swindon
82D Westbury
82E Bristol Barrow Road (to Western Region 1958-1965 ex-LMS shed code 22A)
82F Weymouth (to Southern Region code 71G 1958-1963)
83A Newton Abbot
83B Taunton
83C Exeter
83D Plymouth Laira
83E St Blazey
83F Truro
83G Penzance
84A Wolverhampton Stafford Road
84B Oxley (to London Midland Region, code 2B from 1963-1966)
84C Banbury (to London Midland Region, code 2D from 1963-1966)

84D Leamington (to London Midland Region, code 2L from 1963 -1965)
84E Tyseley (to London Midland Region, code 2A from 1963-1966)
84F Stourbridge (to London Midland Region, code 2C from 1963-1966)
84G Shrewsbury (to London Midland Region, code 6D from 1963-1967)
84K Chester (to London Midland Region, code 6E from 1958-1960)
85A Worcester
85B Gloucester
85C Hereford (86C from 1960-1964)
86C Cardiff Canton (86A from 1960-1962)
86E Severn Tunnel Junction
86G Pontypool Road
87A Neath
87E Landore
87F Llanelly

87G Carmarthern
87H Neyland
87J Goodwick
88B Cardiff East Dock (88L 1962-1963, 88A 1963-1965).

In 1958, and again in 1963, regional boundary changes saw some Western Region depots effectively change regions, however many of these depots still retained an allocation of ex-Great Western locomotives, including *Halls*, many right up until closure. Weymouth was transferred to the Southern region becoming 71G as early as February 1958, but did not lose its Western locomotive allocation until the end of 1962. In 1963 further boundary changes saw ex-Great Western steam depots in the Wolverhampton (84), and Oswestry (89) divisions become part of the London Midland Region.

An early casualty as interested spectators view no. 4909 *Blakesley Hall* on a rather static semi-fast passenger service, seen here at Aller Junction soon after colliding with a goods train on 23 April 1929. It had been completed at Swindon in January 1929 and allocated to Plymouth Laira. The loco had minimal damage and was repaired at Newton Abbot works during the following week. The first fourteen members of the class were initially allocated to Penzance and Plymouth Laira, probably for appraisal purposes.
Great Western Trust

An almost brand new no. 4940 *Ludford Hall* is seen here at Starcross in August 1929 with an up fast service from the South West to Paddington. Completed at Swindon in July 1939 it was allocated from new to Taunton. It returned to Swindon in early August to be fitted with ATC apparatus, as seen here. The first twenty *Halls* were not initially fitted with ATC, but by 1930 all had received it. The *Hall* is coupled to a reconditioned Churchward 3,500 gallon tender no. 2030 that dates from November 1917. The first forty *Halls* left the works with reconditioned Churchward tenders. Great Western Trust

No. 4963 *Rignall Hall* pictured here at Reading in the early 1930s, and pretty much as built. It is coupled to a Collett 4,000 gallon tender no. 2446. These tenders were used on the *Halls* from September 1929, with no. 4958 *Priory Hall* being the first recipient. Notice also the upper lamp bracket attached to the top of the smokebox. This was discontinued in May 1933 when the lamp bracket was moved to a lower position on the front of the smokebox door. Great Western Trust

Looking almost like a model railway scene, Penzance allocated no. 4989 *Cherwell Hall*, crosses Blackwater Viaduct as it approaches Chasewater station in September 1931 with a down local stopping service from Plymouth to Penzance. It is coupled to Collett tender no. 2419. Great Western Trust

During May and June 1932 no. 4932 *Hatherton Hall* was at Swindon Works for testing. It was being used in comparison tests with *Saint* no. 2935 *Caynham Court*, which had been fitted with Rotary Cam Poppet valve gear and new cylinders. No. 4932 is pictured here fitted with a front indicator shelter and is coupled to the GWR Churchward designed Dynamometer car no. 790. Built at Swindon in 1901 the Dynamometer car was renumbered W7W by the Western Region and withdrawn from service in 1961. Great Western Trust

An undated but early 1930s shot of no. 4906 *Bradfield Hall* (Penzance) arriving at Torquay with a down stopping service for Kingswear, again notice the top lamp bracket with red painted lamp. The train comprises a mixture of early Great Western stock including a 6-wheeled K14 Dean passenger van. The stone signal box on the right of the picture was closed on 15 November 1984 and was designated a grade II listed building on 9 April 1986. Great Western Trust

A portrait of no.4966 *Shakenhurst Hall* from Plymouth Laira, as it waits to depart from Exeter St Davids with a down stopping service to Plymouth on 17 April 1933. No. 4966 spent most of its early working life in the South West.
L Hanson/Great Western Trust

No. 5905 *Knowsley Hall* pictured here in Swindon works during an Intermediate Repair in August 1933. It has had the top lampbracket removed from the smokebox, but has not been refitted in the lower position on the smokebox door. The *Hall* is in green livery but has not yet been lined out. Standing alongside is now preserved no. 4965 *Rood Ashton Hall* that was also in at the same time for a HG repair.
Great Western Trust

A through service from Birmingham to Penzance climbs Wellington Bank in Somerset in September 1933. It is hauled by no. 4930 *Hagley Hall* (Oxley) Class no. 4096 *Highclere Castle* (Bristol Bath Road). Great Western Trust

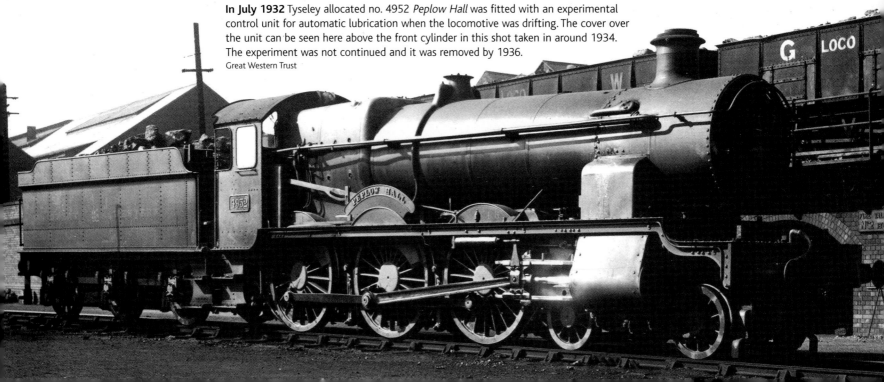

In July 1932 Tyseley allocated no. 4952 *Peplow Hall* was fitted with an experimental control unit for automatic lubrication when the locomotive was drifting. The cover over the unit can be seen here above the front cylinder in this shot taken in around 1934. The experiment was not continued and it was removed by 1936. Great Western Trust

E NOT ALLOWED
RAILWAY
E BRIDGE

LOSTWITHIEL
CHANGE FOR FOWEY

A nicely framed shot of no. 4907 *Broughton Hall* from Penzance depot as it arrives at Lostwithiel on 22 May 1935 with a down stopping service to Penzance. Built in January 1929, it was allocated from new to Penzance. The Fowey branch platform is on the right, behind the signal box.
Great Western Trust

A service from Portsmouth to Birmingham is seen here in around 1935 leaving the West Curve at Reading, hauled by no. 4921 *Eaton Hall* from Oxford. The locomotive is coupled to a reconditioned Churchward 3,500 gallon tender no. 1758. The large train reporting numbers were first introduced by the Great Western in 1934.
Great Western Trust

A nice portrait of no. 4947 *Nanhoran Hall* from Truro as it stands in the yard at Penzance on 25 August 1936. Completed at Swindon in August 1929, the *Hall* is in fully lined GW green with the small GWR roundel on Churchward 3,500 gallon tender no. 2035. The simple design GWR roundel was introduced by the company in 1934. Great Western Trust

Once clearance tests had taken place *Halls* were allowed to work over Southern metals as far as Bournemouth from as early as 1932. Pictured here at Bournemouth MPD yard on 4 October 1936 is no. 5931 *Hatherley Hall* from Old Oak Common. It had probably worked in with an excursion train. M Yarwood/Great Western Trust

Double heading on the South Devon banks, with no. 4947 *Nanhoran Hall,* and *Bulldog* class 4-4-0 no 3342 *Bonaventura* (both Penzance) ascending the 1 in 42 Hemerdon bank with an up service from Penzance on 7 May 1936. The Hemerdon stop board for goods and mineral trains can be seen on the left. M Yarwood/Great Western Trust

Oxley allocated no. 4944 *Middleton Hall* makes a fine sight on a down seven coach semi-fast service at Brent Knoll in 1936. The locomotive is in lined out middle chrome Great Western green, and is coupled to Churchward 3,500 gallon tender no. 1947. Notice the upper lamp bracket has been moved to the smokebox door. Great Western Trust

No. 4979 *Wootton Hall* from Tyseley stands in the centre road at Birmingham Snow Hill on 24 April 1937. Withdrawn from Oxford on 28 September 1963, it was sold to Dai Woodham and subsequently stored at Barry for a number of years. It was resold to the Furness Railway Trust, and is currently being restored at The Appleby Heritage Centre. Great Western Trust

No. 4910 *Blaisdon Hall* from Plymouth Laira, is pictured here in June 1937 after departing from Teignmouth with an up stopping service from Plymouth to Exeter, comprising five coaches and a van. Great Western Trust

Taunton based no. 4954 *Plaish Hall* approaches Dawlish with an up fast service from Plymouth on 29 August 1937. Interestingly, some four years after the practice was abandoned the locomotive still retains its top lamp bracket.

No.5913 *Rushton Hall* from Westbury is pictured here near Frome with a six-coach Bristol to Weymouth service in the summer of 1937. Built at Swindon in June 1931, it is seen here coupled to Collett 4,000 gallon tender no. 2620. Great Western Trust

The *Halls* saw extensive use as pilots over the South Devon banks, and here in the summer of 1937 no. 4906 *Bradfield Hall* (Truro) pilots King Class 4-6-0 no. 6019 *King Henry V* (Laira) over Bank with the 11.05am service from Paddington to Penzance. Notice the white painted headlamps on the Hall. Great Western Trust

No. 5934 *Kneller Hallfrom Didcot*, is pictured here on a parcels service at Kensington Addison Road station on 31 July 1937. It has the GWR roundel on Collett 4,000 gallon tender no. 2561. Great Western Trust

Oak Common allocated No. 4935 *Ketley Hall*, pictured here during an Intermediate Repair in Swindon A shop on 3 January 1938. Of interest on the right is 4300 class Mogul no. 8382, as no. 5382 in June 1920, it received a heavier front end in January 1928. In February 1945 the front end modification was removed it reverted back to no. 5382.
Great Western Trust

Lots of parcels being loaded and unloaded from an unidentified Westbury to Weymouth service, hauled by Weymouth based no. 5949 *Trematon Hall* at Yeovil Pen Mill on 26 July 1939. The Westbury to Weymouth services were a regular turn for a Weymouth based *Hall*. M Yarwood/Great Western Trust

The ill-fated Truro based no. 4911 *Bowden Hall* in the shed yard at Penzance on 23 August 1939. It was coupled at this time to Churchward 3,500 gallon tender no. 2225. In March 1940 it was at Swindon for an Intermediate Repair, the tender was swapped for Collett 4,000 gallon no. 2701. Great Western Trust

For obvious reasons wartime pictures of railway operations are few and far between. In this rare shot, Reading based no. 4914 *Cranmore Hall* seen near Haddenham on 2 June 1940 with a special Dunkirk evacuation train. Operation Dynamo saw some 338,226 troops evacuated from the beaches at Dunkirk between 27 May and 4 June 1940. Almost all were conveyed from the Channel ports by rail, the GWR operated 40 of the 186 special evacuation trains.
C G Stuart/Great Western Trust

The remains of no. 4911 *Bowden Hall* after it was struck by a German bomb at Keyham, Plymouth, on the evening of 29/30 April 1941. The locomotive was subsequently withdrawn, but its Collett 4,000 gallon tender no. 2701 was repaired and put back into service. Great Western Trust

A long parcels train from the south arrives at Shrewsbury hauled by Chester based no. 6941 in September 1945. The locomotive has not yet been named and has blanked out cabside windows. Built in August 1942, it was named *Fillongley Hall* in April 1946. The large signal box at Severn Bridge Junction, built high to give an overall view of the various junctions here, can be seen behind the train.
C G Stuart/Great Western Trust

A rather dirty looking *Modified Hall* no. 6970 from Oxley, waits at Oxford North Junction with an up freight in around 1946. The locomotive is still in wartime black livery with cab side windows blanked out and it has its canvas roof cover rolled up out of the way. It was named *Whaddon Hall* in May 1947. RHG Simpson/Great Western Trust

A bit of a mishap involving *Hall*, no. 6910 *Gossington Hall* from Old Oak Common, seen here lying on its side at Wootton Bassett on 27 June 1946 after being derailed whilst working the 11.50am Paddington to South Wales parcel train. As can be seen, the mostly wooden vehicles are piled up behind the locomotive. Surprisingly the *Hall* suffered only minor damage, and was soon repaired at Swindon. Great Western Trust

Not a lot of health and safety in evidence as no. 5958 *Knolton Hall* from Cardiff Canton, on a down class D express freight service, passes track repairs at Steventon on 3 November 1946. The loco is so dirty that the front number has been outlined in chalk. Obviously the track maintenance crew are not expecting an imminent service on the up main. Today it is probable that all of the lines at this point would be closed for this type of work.
M Yarwood /Great Western Trust

Tyseley allocated no. 5997 *Sparkford Hall* is pictured here at Slough on a down parcels service on 10 June 1947. *Halls* continued to be built at Swindon throughout the war, no. 5997 being turned out in June 1940.
Great Western Trust

No. 3902 *Northwick Hall* (4948) from Bristol St Phillips Marsh stands at Salisbury in 1947 with a Portsmouth to Bristol service. It was converted to burn oil in May 1947, but did not last for long as an oil burner, being restored to coal burning in September 1948.
Great Western Trust

A rather grubby looking no. 4903 *Astley Hall* from Oxford is pictured here at Reading with an up freight on 12 March 1948. According to the records it is running with rebuilt Dean tender no. 1459, that dates from August 1900. Great Western Trust

With a full tender, no 5925 *Eastcote Hall* from Westbury, departs from Newbury on 12 March 1948 with the 10.45am five coach stopping service from Paddington to Devizes and Trowbridge. M Yarwood/Great Western Trust

An unidentified stopping service from Paddington to Birmingham, hauled by no. 5995 *Wick Hall* from Woverhampton Stafford Road, is seen here approaching Wheatley (Oxon) on the single line Oxford to Princes Risborough branch on Sunday, 16 May 1948. The service was being diverted via Oxford due to Sunday engineering work between Princes Risborough and Aynho Junction
C G Stuart/Great Western Trust

No. 6983 *Otterington Hall* was completed at Swindon on 13 February 1948, just six weeks after Nationalisation. At this time there was a certain amount of uncertainty over the new livery for the *Hall* Class locomotives, and no. 6983 was turned out in a GW style lined green livery, with British Railways in Great Western style lettering painted on Hawksworth 4,000 gallon tender no. 4042. The *Hall* has the small W (signifying Western Region) painted under the cab numberplate and still retains its loco number on the front bufferbeam. It is seen here at Westbourne Park on 20 May 1948 on empty stock.
C G Stuart/Great Western Trust

An up parcels service from the Reading area, comprising an assortment of stock passes through Ealing Broadway hauled by no. 5933 *Kingsway Hall* (Reading) minus its safety valve cover, on 20 June 1948. Notice also what appears to be a photographer perched high on wooden steps on the up platform. C G Stuart/Great Western Trust

No. 6978 *Haroldstone Hall* accelerates away from Salisbury with a ten coach Portsmouth to Cardiff service on 6 July 1948. Although a sub shed of Westbury, the records show that no. 6978 was allocated to Salisbury at this time.
M Yarwood/Great Western Trust

Some poor coal being burnt here as no. 6979 *Helperly Hall* pilots Worcester based no. 5017 *St Donat's Castle* on a Paddington to Wolverhampton service via Oxford at Westbourne Park on 31 August 1948. No. 6979 spent the whole of its working life allocated to Banbury from where it was withdrawn in February 1965.
C G Stuart/Great Western Trust

The now preserved no. 6989 *Wightwick Hall* from Hereford, emerges from Ledbury Tunnel as it enters Ledbury with a through service from Paddington to Hereford on 10 September 1948. The *Hall* is in GW style lined green livery, with its number painted on the front buffer beam, and with 'British Railways' in Swindon style lettering on Hawksworth tender no. 4048.
G G Stuart/Great Western Trust

A view of no. 6916 *Misterton Hall* ex-works condition at Worcester in October 1948. The locomotive and tender are freshly painted in the new BR mixed traffic lined black, but with a plain unlettered tender. Whilst in the works it was fitted with a smokebox number plate, but it still retains the WOS (Worcester) on the front frame, although records indicate that it was allocated to Hereford at this time. Great Western Trust

In ex-works condition after a HG repair at Swindon, Old Oak Common allocated no. 5938 *Stanley Hall* passes through Acton on 22 May 1950 with the 6.00pm service from Paddington to Weymouth. This service ran via Westbury and Yeovil. C G Stuart/Great Western Trust

The new mixed traffic black livery can be seen to good effect on no. 5954 *Faendre Hall* as it waits to depart from Oxford in July 1950 with the Saturdays only (SO) Wolverhampton to Margate service. The *Hall* has received its new brass smoke box number plate, and its home shed BAN (Banbury) can be seen on front frame.
Great Western Trust

Modified Hall no. 7902 *Eaton Mascot Hall* speeds past Shrivenham on 5 August 1950 with the Saturdays only 10am service from Torquay to Wolverhampton via Oxford. No. 7902 was built in March 1949, and spent the whole of its working life allocated to Old Oak Common, from where it was withdrawn on 1 June 1964. Great Western Trust

The 4.45pm service from Paddington to Worcester and Hereford, hauled by no. 7920 *Coney Hall* (85A), passes Kennington on its approach to Oxford on 6 July 1951. R H G Simpson/Great Western Trust

An unidentified service from Birmingham to Cardiff is seen here at Stratford-upon-Avon on 8 September 1951, hauled by Cardiff Canton (86C) based no. 6946 *Heatherden Hall*. The lococomotive is in BR mixed traffic lined black livery and has the short lived experiment of red backed name and numberplates.
Great Western Trust

No. 6994 *Baggrave Hall* in the shed yard at Taunton on 17 September 1951. The locomotive is in mixed traffic lined black, and has been fitted with a smokebox numberplate and an (83C) Exeter shed plate. The Collett 4,000 gallon tender no. 2843 is still in post-war GWR livery.

A nice low level shot of no.4924 Eydon Hall Oxley (84B) as it
approaches Seer Green on 5 July 1952 with the 10.10am through
service from Birmingham Snow Hill to Margate. The train comprises
ex-Southern Railway green stock.
Brian Morrison

The 8.45am SO cross country service from Kingswear to Bradford is pictured here at Stratford-upon-Avon on 26 July 1952, hauled by no. 7916 *Mobberley Hall* (83A). During the summer months many cross country services to and from the Midlands and the South West used the Cheltenham - Stratford - Birmingham route.
Great Western Trust

Pictured here in its final form, no. 4900 *Saint Martin* (85A) stands at Old Oak Common in May 1953. It is painted in BR mixed traffic lined black with lion and wheel emblem on Collett 4,000 gallon tender no. 2835. No. 4900 had been fitted with outside steam pipes and a new front end at Swindon in December 1948, but still retains its lower pitched boiler.
Great Western Trust

A super panoramic shot of Swindon based no. 5934 *Kneller Hall* piloting an unidentified *Castle* on its approach to Sapperton Tunnel on 10 September 1949 with the 12.10pm service from Cheltenham St James to Paddington.
M Yarwood/Great Western Trust

No. 6990 *Witherslack Hall* (81A) stands alongside the coaling plant at Old Oak Common on 28 November 1954. Built at Swindon by BR in March 1948, unusually both the locomotive and tender no. 2830 are still in post-war Great Western lined green livery. R C Riley

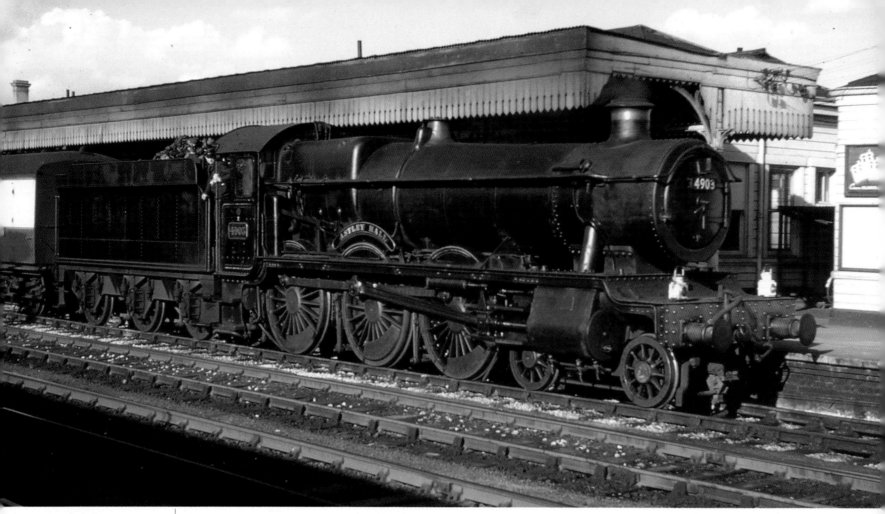

No. 4903 *Astley Hall* (81F) stands at Oxford on 29 September 1956 with the 2.38pm service from Leamington. The locomotive is in BR mixed traffic lined black, but with no emblem on the tender. R C Riley

A portrait of no. 5959 *Mawley Hall* (83G) in BR mixed traffic black livery at Old Oak Common in November 1956.
R C Riley

No. 4955 *Plaspower Hall* (83A) passes milepost 326 near Penzandane on its way out of Penzance with the 1.20pm through service from Penzance to Paddington, comprising just four coaches and a van on 11 May 1959. M Mensing

Modified Hall no. 6971 *Athelhampton Hall* (84E) runs through Shirley Station on the North Warwickshire line on Saturday, 29 August 1959 with the 3.45pm service from Birmingham Snow Hill to Swansea High Street. M Mensing

No. **5909** *Newton Hall* (87F) is pictured here at Tyseley Station on Saturday, 29 August 1959 with a through service from South Wales to Birmingham Snow Hill via the North Warwickshire line. M Mensing

An interesting shot of no. 5919 *Worsley Hall* traversing the single line section of the Severn Beach to Pilning branch at New Passage Halt with an Avonmouth to South Wales (via Pilning) Banana train on 28 September 1959. The *Hall* will run around its train at Pilning. M Mensing

No. **7900** *St Peters Hall* (81F) is pictured here at Kennington Junction in March 1961 with a through service from Wolverhampton to the South East. It is running with Collet tender no. 2746. Notice also the front smokebox numberplate has a red background. Dr G Smith/ courtesy Mrs B Smith

The fireman of no. 6947 *Helmingham Hall* (85A) looks back at his train as it awaits to depart from Oxford, with the 10am Paddington to Worcester Shrub Hill service in March 1961.
Dr G Smith /courtesy Mrs B Smith

Out of use in the gas works siding at Swindon on 9 April 1961 is no. 4927 *Farnborough Hall*. Allocated to Neath (87A), it had returned to Swindon for further attention after receiving a HG Heavy General repair the previous month.
C G Stuart/Great Western Trust

No. 4975 *Umberslade Hall* (83A) pilots *Warship* Class no. D600 *Active* out of Totnes with a Paddington to Plymouth service on 20 June 1961.
A E Doyle

No. 4939 *Littleton Hall* (81E) rounds the sharp curve at Leamington Spa General on 7 October 1961 with a down Class F mixed freight service. M Mensing

No. 5921 *Bingley Hall* (82D) stands in the locomotive yard at Westbury on 25 December 1961. Also in view are ex-Great Western 2-8-0 no. 3845 (86C), and 2-6-0 no. 6319 (83D). Over the years Westbury had a large allocation of *Halls*, in 1959, for example, there were nine Collett and four *Modified Halls* working from the shed. CG Stuart/Great Western Trust

Modified Hall no. 6963 *Throwley Hall* is pictured here at Leamington Spa General on a frosty 27 December 1961. It has the narrow diameter chimney and improved draughting. Allocated at this time to Old Oak Common, it is coupled to Hawksworth tender no. 4069. A E Doyle

No. 4980 *Wrottesley Hall* (82B) is pictured here leaving the down goods loop at Witham on 24 February 1962 with a down mixed freight. It is coupled to Hawksworth tender no. 4097.
P A Fry/Great Western Trust

A down class F mixed freight service probably from Acton yard passes West Ealing on 16 March 1962, hauled by no. 5945 *Leckhampton Hall* (81C).
C G Stuart/Great Western Trust

An up class H mixed freight crosses Chester Line Junction as it pulls into Didcot on 27 March 1962, hauled by no. 5986 *Arbury Hall* (81E).
C G Stuart/Great Western Trust

No. 6920 *Barningham Hall* (81A) is pictured here at Croes Newydd with a Birkenhead to Paddington service on 23 April 1962. It was running at this time with Hawksworth tender no. 4101.
A E Doyle

An interesting shot of no. 5905 *Knowsley Hall* at Gloucester on 13 March 1962. It was in Swindon during January 1962 for Heavy Intermediate repair. The records show that it was then placed in store at Swindon until it was allocated to Gloucester on 14 February 1962. It is pictured here at Gloucester still apparently in store and with its chimney covered. It was re-allocated to Goodwick on 9 July. C G Stuart/Great Western Trust

A fine portrait of no. 4932 *Hatherton Hall* (83B) as it stands on shed at Plymouth Laira on 29 April 1962.
CG Stuart/Great Western Trust

Another shot taken at Plymouth Laira on the same day shows the now preserved no. 4920 *Dumbleton Hall* (83D), which had recently left Swindon after a heavy general repair. No. 4920 was the oldest *Hall* to survive on the Western Region. Constructed at Swindon in March 1929, it was withdrawn on 31 December 1965.
GCG Stuart/Great Western Trust

The 8.35am service from Newcastle to Bournemouth West calls at Banbury on 14 May 1962, hauled by no. 7905 *Fowey Hall* (84C), coupled to Collett tender no. 2768. The whole train comprises ER stock, except the ex-Southern Railway 4 wheel horse van.
CG Stuart/Great Western Trust

Not long out of Swindon works after a Heavy Intermediate repair, no. 6942 *Eshton Hall* (81A) plods along on a down mixed freight near Wednesbury, West Midlands, in June 1962. This stretch of the old Great Western main line now forms part of the tramlink between Birmingham and Wolverhampton
M Hale/Great Western Trust

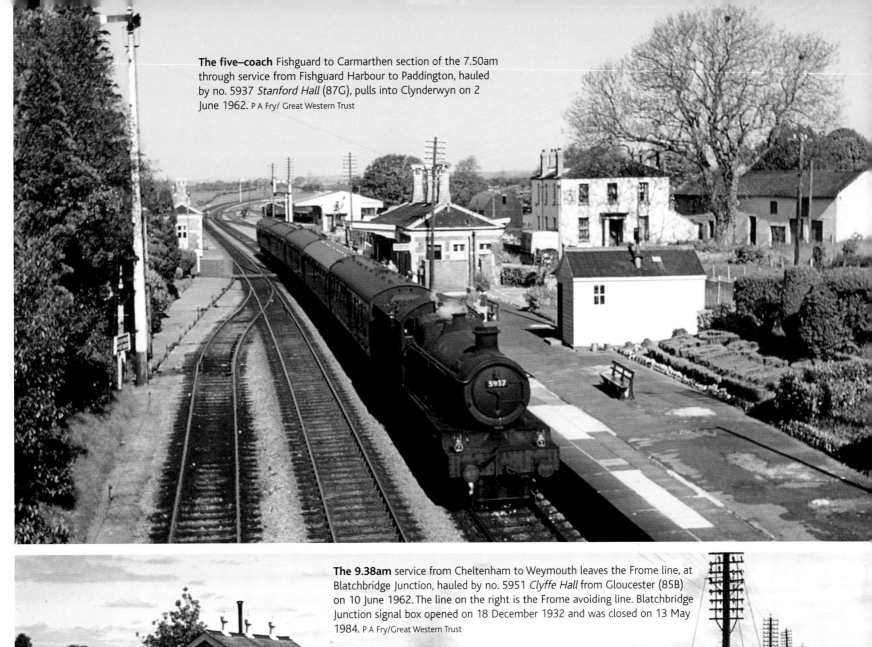

The five–coach Fishguard to Carmarthen section of the 7.50am through service from Fishguard Harbour to Paddington, hauled by no. 5937 *Stanford Hall* (87G), pulls into Clynderwyn on 2 June 1962. P A Fry/ Great Western Trust

The 9.38am service from Cheltenham to Weymouth leaves the Frome line, at Blatchbridge Junction, hauled by no. 5951 *Clyffe Hall* from Gloucester (85B) on 10 June 1962. The line on the right is the Frome avoiding line. Blatchbridge Junction signal box opened on 18 December 1932 and was closed on 13 May 1984. P A Fry/Great Western Trust

No. 6998 *Burton Agnes Hall* (81A) on a Wolverhampton to Weymouth excursion is seen here on the Frome loop line on 22 June 1962. On 2 January 1966 no. 6998 hauled the 2.10pm Bournemouth to York service between Oxford and Banbury, the last official steam passenger turn on the Western Region. It had been officially withdrawn from Oxford on 31 December 1965. It was then sold to the Great Western Society, and can now be seen at Didcot Railway Centre.
C G Stuart /Great Western Trust

Seen here shunting at Swindon on 7 August 1962 is no. 6986 *Rydal Hall* from Bristol St Phillips Marsh (82B). It is coupled to Collett 4,000 gallon tender no. 2619. The *Hall* has the narrow chimney and improved draughting. C G Stuart/Great Western Trust

A summer Saturday Holiday extra from the West Midlands to Bournemouth, hauled by no. 4983 *Albert Hall* (81A), comes off the Reading line at Basingstoke on 10 August 1962. No. 4983 is not quite what it seems. Records show that it was withdrawn from Old Oak in December 1963. After lanquishing in the yard at Barry for a number of years, sold to Woodham Bros, from there it went to Tyseley and has since been restored back to running order as no. 4965 *Rood Ashton Hall*. See main text for an explanation.
C G Stuart/Great Western Trust

The 11.37am service from Portsmouth Harbour to Bristol, hauled by no. 5999 *Wollaton Hall* (82D), passes the neat and tidy lineside allotments at Oldfield Park on 8 September 1962.
PA Fry/Great Western Trust

The return leg of the Ian Allan 'Somerset and Dorset' rail tour departs from Bath Green Park en route to Cheltenham on 22 September 1962, hauled by no. 4992 *Crosby Hall* (82B), running at this date with Hawksworth tender no. 4035. On the left is the ex-Somerset and Dorset locomotive depot. P A Fry /Great Western Trust

No. 4954 *Plaish Hall* (84E) speeds past Madeley Junction with a down class C freight on 29 September 1962. The line on the left is the single line branch to Lightmoor Junction. M Hale /Great Western Trust

The four coach Hereford portion of the 09.15am service from Paddington is seen here near Malvern Wells on 13 October 1962, hauled by no. 7926 *Willey Hall* (85A).
P A Fry/Great Western Trust

Standing in the winter sunshine at Stroud on Christmas Eve, 24 December 1962, is no. 4930 *Hagley Hall* (82C) with the 9.40am stopping service from Swindon to Gloucester. The *Hall* has since been preserved, and is currently at the Severn Valley Railway.
P A Fry/Great Western Trust

Another shot taken on 24 December 1962 shows no. 6927 *Lilford Hall* (81F) as it speeds through Ledbury with an up 'empty stock'.
CGStuart/Great Western Trust

No. 6928 *Underlay Hall* (86G) makes a fine sight as it rounds the curve at Red Hill Junction near Hereford on 11 February 1963, with a class C freight comprising mainly empty cattle trucks.
M Hale/Great Western Trust

A good portrait of no. 7923 *Speke Hall* (81C) in the shed yard at Southall on 17 March 1963. Its tender is piled high ready for its next duty. It had recently left Swindon after a Heavy Intermediate repair, and is coupled to Collett tender no. 2619.
C G Stuart/Great Western Trust

Looking in poor external condition, the now preserved no. 5900 *Hinderton Hall* (82B) passes Gloucester in March 1963, with a ballast train from the Bristol area. The ATC apparatus on the front of the loco can be seen to good effect. No. 5900 was withdrawn from service on 2 December 1963, and is now kept at Didcot Railway Centre.
A E Doyle

No. 7911 *Lady Margaret Hall* (81F) awaits its next turn of duty as it stands in the yard at Oxford on 28 March 1963. It has the narrow pattern chimney and improved draughting, and is coupled to Collett tender no. 2751. It was allocated to Old Oak Common for just a year, before moving to Oxford, where it spent the rest of its working life.
C G Stuart/Great Western Trust

The three-coach Pembroke Dock portion of the 8.30am service from Pembroke Dock to Paddington is pictured here at Whitland on 22 April 1963, hauled by no. 6984 *Owsden Hall* (87H). It is coupled to Collett tender no. 2310. Extra coaches will be added at both Carmarthen and Swansea.
A E Doyle

6916 *Misterton Hall* from Shrewsbury (84G) is pictured here under repair in the locomotive works at Wolverhampton Stafford Road on 26 May 1963. It was in the works for a Heavy Classified repair. In the background is its Hawksworth tender no. 4048. Wolverhampton works was closed completely on 1 June 1964, the last locomotive left after repair on 11 February 1964.
M Hale/Great Western Trust

The 11.15am service from Paddington to Worcester and Hereford speeds through West Ealing on 1 June 1963 hauled by no. 7920 *Coney Hall* (85A). This was the last full year of steam traction on the Worcester services. CG Stuart/Great Western Trust

No. **6965** *Thirlestaine Hall* (87F) climbs up the bank from St Andrews Junction, Birmingham, with a heavy coal train on 29 July 1963. It was coupled at this time to Hawksworth tender no. 4041. M Mensing

A service from Paddington to Worcester and Hereford is pictured here at Campden Bank in July 1963, hauled by *Modified Hall* no. 6992 *Arborfield Hall* (85A). It was coupled at the date to Collett tender no. 2890. Great Western Trust

An up freight probably en route to Banbury yard, hauled by no. 6911 *Holker Hall* (2D, passes slowly through Birmingham Snow Hill in August 1963.
M Hale/Great Western Trust

No. 5932 *Haydon Hall* (81D) arrives at a wet Yeovil Pen Mill on 7 September 1963 with the 7.05am service from Birmingham Snow Hill to Weymouth.
P A Fry/Great Western Trust

No. 6976 *Graythwaite Hall* (84C), in sparkling ex-works condition after a Heavy Casual repair, stands outside the works at Swindon on 26 January 1964. It is coupled to Collett tender no.4018. It has received the narrower design chimney and improved draughting. This was signified by the letters ID painted on the frame behind the front bufferbeam. Also seen here to good effect is the red route D classification, and also the X that signifies that this locomotive can take heavier loads. This was its final visit to Swindon as it was withdrawn in October 1965.
C G Stuart/Great Western Trust

No. 5955 *Garth Hall* (81F) and *Warship* Class 42 no. D858 Valorous are seen here at Patchway on 29 February 1964 with the 9.50am through service from Liverpool Lime Street to Plymouth. The photographer has not indicated as to whether or not the *Warship* had broken down.
P A Fry/Great Western Trust

There is no doubt that no. 6988 *Swithland Hall* (82D) has seen better days as it stands in the winter sunshine at Devizes with the 3.15pm service from Westbury to Reading on 7 March 1964. It was withdrawn from Reading in September 1964. P A Fry/Great Western Trust

A down Class C mixed freight departs from Wolverhampton LL on 11 April 1964, hauled by no. 5990 *Dorford Hall* from Banbury (2D). Withdrawn in January 1965, it was cut up by J. Friswell at Banbury MPD. M Hale/Great Western Trust

On a clear but crisp 4 May 1964, no. 5927 *Guild Hall* from Tyseley (2A) speeds past Wolvercote siding, north of Oxford, with a northbound class C freight. A E Doyle

An up freight from South Wales passes through Gloucester Central on 16 May 1964, hauled by the now preserved no. 6960 *Raveningham Hall* (81F). It was withdrawn from Oxford just a few weeks later on 1 June 1964. It is currently on the West Somerset Railway. P A Fry /Great Western Trust

No. 6911 *Holker Hall* (2D) stands at Banbury on 16 July 1964 after arriving with the 5.25pm stopping service from Oxford. Although part of the London Midland Region, Banbury still had an allocation of six *Halls* and two *Modified Halls* at this time. D Tuck

No. 4992 *Crosby Hall* (82B) stands at Weymouth on 3 September 1964 with the 5.20pm service to Paddington. No. 4992 was withdrawn from Bristol Barrow Road in April 1965. M Hale/Great Western Trust

No. 7927 *Willington Hall* from Cardiff East Dock is seen here near Upwey with a Weymouth service on 4 September 1964. Withdrawn in December 1965, the loco survived the cutters torch and has, in recent years, been used as a donor locomotive for the Hawksworth County project.
M Hale/Great Western Trust

No. 4933 *Himley Hall* (84G) passes through Evershot on the Yeovil to Weymouth line with the 11.05am service from Weymouth Town to Wolverhampton LL on 5 September 1964. Notice the upper quadrant signal. This ex-Great Western line became part of the Southern Region in 1958.
P A Fry/Great Western Trust

No. 6963 *Throwley Hall* (81D) backs out of Paddington with the empty stock of the 08.52am service from Oxford on Saturday, 10 October 1964. This was the last scheduled steam hauled passenger service from Oxford to Paddington. D W Tuck

No. 6900 *Abney Hall* (82E) is seen here being lifted after a derailment whilst working an up freight near Radley on 12 October 1964. The *Hall* was not repaired and was subsequently withdrawn during the same month. D W Tuck

An up coal train hauled by a nameless and in poor external condition no. 4962 *Ragley Hall* (81E), seen here approaching Bentley Heath Crossing on 13 August 1965. A number of the class had their smokebox hinges painted white at this time.
M Mensing

Deviod of any identification other than a chalked number on the cabside, no. 7922, formerly *Salford Hall,* (81C) waits for the road at Basingstoke on a down engineering train, possibly to Eastleigh yard, in October 1965. It was withdrawn just two months later.
Great Western Trust

No. 6999 *Capel Dewi Hall* is pictured here at Oxford in late December 1965. Looking rather the worse for wear, it had the rather dubious distinction as being the very last steam station pilot at Oxford. The *Hall* arrived at Oxford from Severn Tunnel Junction during the same month, and was withdrawn when the shed closed on 31 December 1965. A E Doyle

An up class F freight hauled by no. 5907 *Marble Hall* from Tyseley (84E) is pictured here near Denham (Bucks) in April 1953. The locomotive is in mixed traffic lined black with red backed name and cabside numberplates. Brian Morrison

A parcels train of mixed stock, probably from the Reading area, arrives at Paddington on 29 April 1953, hauled by no. 5962 *Wantage Hall* (81A). Notice the first vehicle on the train, which is a 6-wheel type K 4 Dean brake van dating from 1896. The second vehicle is an ex-Southern Railway eight wheel passenger van.
P Kelley

The guard poses for the photographer alongside Tyseley (84E) allocated Modified Hall no. 6971 *Athelhampton Hall* here at Barry Island as it prepares to take a Sunday excursion back to Birmingham on 7 June 1953. Barry Island was a popular destination for excursion trains from the Midlands. E Mountford/Great Western Trust

An unidentified ten-coach down excursion approaches Wolvercote Junction, north of Oxford on 13 July 1953 hauled by Tyseley (84E) allocated no. 5900 *Hinderton Hall*. Today *Hinderton Hall* is kept at Didcot Railway Centre.
E Bruton/Great Western Trust

The 12.15pm SO service from Kingswear to Wolverhampton is seen here near Bearley on the North Warwickshire line on 1 August 1953, hauled by no. 6958 *Oxburgh Hall* from *St Phillips Marsh* (82B). 6958 was the last of the Collett *Halls* to be built, being completed at Swindon in April 1943. It is seen here coupled to Hawksworth 4,000 gallon tender no. 4040.
Great Western Trust

No. 4932 *Hatherton Hall* (83B) stands at Taunton on 22 August 1953 with the 10.20am Saturdays only cross country service from Kingswear to Crewe via Bristol and Cheltenham.
Great Western Trust

Some *Halls* had a long association with one depot. Pictured here at Goodwick (87J), its home shed, is no. 5908 *Moreton Hall.* Built at Swindon in June 1931, it was allocated to Goodwick from 13 January 1933 until 17 January 1962. It was withdrawn from Bristol St Phillips Marsh on 29 July 1963. *Halls* allocated to West Wales depots were rare visitors in the London area.
Great Western Trust

Seen here climbing hard up Sapperton bank in April 1954 is no. 5951 *Clyffe Hall* (85B) with the 2.10pm service from Cheltenham to Swindon.
Great Western Trust

A great shot of now preserved no. 6998 *Burton Agnes Hall* (86C) as it speeds through Sonning on 19 April 1954 with a fast service from Cardiff to Paddington. At this time it was running with a Collett 4,000 gallon tender no. 2914.
Great Western Trust

The very simple BR mixed traffic lined black livery can be seen to good effect on no. 6938 *Corndean Hall* (83C), pictured here in the works yard at Swindon on 20 October 1954 after a HG repair. It is coupled to Hawksworth 4,000 gallon tender no. 4120. This was the last year that this livery was used on the *Halls*, as from the summer of 1955 4-6-0 locomotives passing through the works were turned out in the new British Railways Western Region fully lined middle chrome green livery. Great Western Trust

The crew prepare no. 5952 *Cogan Hall* for its next turn of duty at its home shed in Penzance (83G) in April 1955. The *Hall* is in mixed traffic lined black and shows to good effect the X above the cabside numberplate, which denoted that the loco was able to handle heavier loads. Great Western Trust

A nice view of no. 7924 *Thornycroft Hall Iver* (Bucks) with a Kensington to Whitland milk train on 25 June 1955, to Westbury (82D). It is seen here running with Collett 4,000 gallon tender no. 2437. Bulk milk trains using 3,000 gallon capacity wagons had been introduced by the Great Western during 1927. P H Kelley

The Saturdays only 7.43am service from Nottingham to Plymouth, comprising a variety of ex-LMS rolling stock, arrives at Exeter St Davids in June 1955 hauled by no. 6954 *Lotherton Hall* from Bristol (82A).
Great Western Trust

The ex-oil burner no. 5955 *Garth Hall* (87E) stands at Carmarthen on 27 June 1955 after arriving with a stopping service from Swansea. It is coupled to Hawksworth 4,000 gallon tender no. 4093. Great Western Trust

No. 6906 *Chicheley Hall* (84C) approaches Reading West, via the West Curve on the 10am Saturdays only Bradford to Poole service in July 1955. The train comprises a mixture of Midland and Eastern Region stock. 6906 was allocated to Banbury for the whole of its working life, new in November 1940, until withdrawal in April 1965. Great Western Trust

The **08.05am** service from Paignton to Manchester, hauled by no. 5971 *Merevale Hall* (85A), waits to depart from Bristol Temple Meads on 30 July 1955. No. 5971 was one of the last of the *Collett Halls* to work on the Western Region, being withdrawn from Oxford on 31 December 1965.
Great Western Trust.

A rather dirty looking no. 6948 *Holbrooke Hall* (86C) is seen here at Enbourne Junction Newbury with the 11.35am stopping service from Reading to Trowbridge on 1 August 1955. It is running here with Hawksworth tender no. 4084. The line in the foreground is the Didcot, Newbury and Southampton line to Winchester and Southampton.
M Yarwood/Great Western Trust

With a tender full of coal Cardiff Canton (86C) based no. 5925 *Eastcote Hall* departs from Cardiff with a service from Paddington to Swansea on 21 August 1955. On the left is the large stone goods depot at Cardiff Canton.
D Penney/Great Western Trust

A **down** mixed class F freight speeds past Huntercombe Lane Taplow on 25 February 1956, hauled by no. 5906 *Lawton Hall* (81D). At this time is was running with Hawksworth 4,000 gallon tender no. 4109. Mark Yarwood/Great Western Trust

No. **4908** *Broome Hall* from Penzance (83G) departs from Bodmin Road with the down 'Cornishman' the 09.00am service from Wolverhampton Low Level to Penzance on 11 June 1956. M Mensing

The late running eight-coach down 'Cornishman' service from Wolverhampton Low Level to Penzance, hauled by no. 5972 *Olton Hall* (83G), is seen here approaching Treverrin Tunnel on the climb up from Lostwithiel on 13 June 1956. Notice on the right the newly installed but not yet in use colour light signal.
M Mensing

Pictured here at Newport on 26 June 1956 is Hereford (85C) based no. 6916 *Misterton Hall*, with a service from Hereford. It was running with Hawksworth 4,000 gallon tender no. 4042. The large building behind the main station entrance is the ex-Great Western Newport Divisional Headquarters.
Great Western Trust

An unidentified down service from Paddington to Plymouth, pictured at Exeter St Davids in August 1956, hauled by no. 4997 *Eldon Hall* (84B), class 2-8-0 no. 4700 from Old Oak Common. The Churchward 4700 class saw regular use during the summer months on relief passenger services to and from the South West. P Ward/Great Western Trust

A long parcels service for the London area departs from Wolverhampton Low Level in the summer of 1956, hauled by Didcot (81E) based no. 6952 *Kimberley Hall*. Notice on the left the ex-Great Western auto coach, also the line diverging away on the right is the ex-LMSR/Midland Railway line to Walsall and Bescot.
M Hale/Great Western Trust

An unidentified cross country service, possibly *The Cornishman* passes Henley in Arden on 8 September 1956, hauled by no. 4904 *Binnegar Hall* from (84E) Grange - 6-0 6804 Brockington Grange from Bristol St Phillips March (82B). Great Western Trust

No. 5921 *Bingley Hall* from Newport Ebbw Junction (86A) receives finishing touches from the paint crew at Caerphilly works on Thursday, 10 January 1957. It had visited the works for a heavy intermediate (HI) repair and was the first *Hall* to be turned out from Caerphilly in fully lined BR green livery, notice, however, that it still retains the lion and wheel emblem on the tender.
E Mountford/Great Western Trust

Standing in the yard at Swindon works on Sunday, 26 May 1957 after a Heavy General repair is no. 4932 *Hatherton Hall* (83B). It is has been shunted up to what appears to be a British Railways Standard type 4725 gallon tender. Also in view, from left to right, are no. 4920 *Dumbleton Hall*, which had also received a HG repair, 2-6-2T no. 5532, and ex-TVR 0-6-2T no. 349. Just in view on the left is Rodbourne Lane signal box; this box opened on 25 August 1912 and closed on 1 March 1968. E Mountford/Great Western Trus

Against the backdrop of Wenlock Edge, Banbury, (84C) allocated no. 5930 *Hannington Hall* passes Stretton Halt en route to Shrewsbury with the 4.20pm stopping service from Hereford on Whit on Monday, 10 June 1957. All Stretton Halt was opened by the Great Western on 29 February 1936 and was closed to passengers on 9 June 1958. M Mensing

On the same day, and in sparkling ex-works condition after a heavy general (HG) repair at Swindon, no. 7922 *Salford Hall* (84K) passes Church Stretton station with a through service from Cardiff to Birkenhead. M Mensing

The 09.15am cross country service from Margate to Wolverhampton, comprising green ex-Southern stock and hauled by no. 5932 *Haydon Hall* (81A), passes through Swan Village en route to Wolverhampton Low Level in June 1957. In the background is the Junction South signal box and in the foreground the branch to Great Bridge and Dudley. Great Western Trust

Modified Hall no. 6973 *Bricklehampton Hall* (81A) prepares to depart from Maidenhead on 16 February 1958 with the 12.33pm stopping service from Paddington to Reading. B W Leslie/Great Western Trust

On a clear winter morning in 1958 the 1.30pm ironstone train from Banbury Ironstone sidings to Margam, South Wales, climbs Hatton Bank, hauled by no. 4923 *Evenley Hall* from Swansea Llandore (87E) and banked by no. 7908 *Henshall Hall* Tyseley (84E). This service travelled via Hatton South Junction, Stratford-upon-Avon and Honeybourne. Production of iron ore from the Oxfordshire field ceased on 30 September 1967. Great Western Trust

No. 6948 *Holbrooke Hall* minus its shedplate, arrives at Inn Station on Monday, 7 April 1958 with the 11.00am service from Newport to Hereford. The *Hall* is coupled to Hawksworth 4,000 gallon tender no. 4079. At this time no. 6948 was on a short-term allocation to Hereford. Notice the low level platforms at this station. M Mensing

An up class H mixed freight, probably for the London area, runs through Birmingham Snow Hill on 29 April 1958, hauled by no. 4994 *Downton Hall* (81E). L Hanson/Great Western Trust

Halls **were** regular performers on many of the cross country services over the old Great Central route via Banbury, Rugby, and often as far as Leicester Central. Pictured here is no. 4924 *Eydon Hall* (84C) as it approaches Rugby Central with the 11.16am Bournemouth West to Newcastle service on 26 May 1958. M Mensing

No. 6950 *Kingsthorpe Hall* outside its home shed, Worcester, in May 1958. The three-road brick shed seen here was probably opened around 1852. A long-serving *Worcester Hall*, no. 6950, was allocated from new in December 1942, remaining until 1961, after which it was allocated away from Carmarthen. *Worcester* was one of the last strongholds of Western Region, officially closing in December 1965. Great Western Trust

Spotters admire no. 4918 *Dartington Hall* (82A) as it stands at Didcot on 10 June 1958 after arriving with a service from Swindon. The *Hall* is on an ex-works running in turn after a Heavy Intermediate (HI) repair at Swindon. Standing at the adjacent platform is 4300 class 2-6-0 Mogul no. 5397 (81E) with a what appears to be a fast service to Paddington.
J D Edwards

No. 7916 *Mobberley Hall* (83A) runs through Saltash Station on 7 August 1958 with the six-coach 1.20pm service from Penzance to Paddington.
P A Fry/Great Western Trust

The *Cornish* *Riviera* *Express*, the 10.30am service from Paddington to Penzance, stands at Newton Abbot on 10 August 1958, hauled by no. 4971 *Stanway Hall* (83B). The photographer has noted that it is waiting for a pilot loco.
PAFry/Great Western Trust

A high level view of the terminus at Penzance shows no. 5972 *Olton Hall* from Laira (83D) departing with the 10.30am 'Cornishman' service to Wolverhampton on 12 August 1958. In the background is 9400 class 0-6-0PT no. 8409 (83G) on station pilot duty.
J Way/Great Western Trust

No. **5996** *Mytton Hall* (81C) passes Brewham Siganl Box on 16 August 1958 with an unidentified down service from Paddington to the South West. The *Hall* is in spotless condition after receiving a recent Heavy Intermediate (HI) repair at Caerphilly Works. Great Western Trust

The 10.10am service from Weymouth to Birmingham via Oxford, departs from Leamington Spa on 16 August 1958, hauled by no. 5985 *Mostyn Hall* (84E). Over the years many of the *Collett Halls* were paired with Hawksworth 4,000 gallon tenders; this one being no. 4051. Brian Morrison.

No. **4986** *Wrottesley Hall* (82A) approaches Stratford upon Avon on 16 August 1958 with the 10.35am cross country service from Paignton to Wolverhampton. Standing in the adjacent loop on a down freight is ex-Great Western 5100 class 2-6-2T no. 5163 (84E). Brian Morrison

The sad sight of the prototype *Hall*, no. 4900 *Saint Martin*, as it awaits its fate outside C shop at Swindon in April 1959. It had been officially withdrawn from Swindon (82C) on 3 April 1959 after fifty-two years in service having completed a total of 2,092,500 miles as both a *Saint* and *Hall*.
R H G Simpson/Great Western Trust

Reading (81D) based no. 5901 *Hazel Hall* stops at Tilehurst on 26 April 1959 with a Thames Valley stopping service from Didcot to Paddington. The station staff have obviously taken great pride in their station, how neat and tidy it all looks.
M Hale/Great Western Trust

An up cup final special from Wolverhampton to Wembley, hauled by no. 4957 *Postlip Hall* from Oxley (84B), speeds through Cholsey and Moulsford on 4 May 1959. The cup final that year was played between Wolverhampton Wanderers and Blackburn. The result Wolves 3 Blackburn 0 meant the Wolves fans had a happy trip home. C G Stuart/Great Western Trust

In sparkling ex-works condition no. 4955 *Plaspower Hall* (83A) backs its five-coach train out of Penzance after arriving with the 7.35am stopping service from Newton Abbot on 12 May 1959. M Mensing

No. 7907 *Hart Hall* from St Phillips Marsh (82B) gets a lot of attention as it passes Bedminster Park, Bristol, with a down class E express freight on 19 October 1959. Great Western Trust

The 12.20pm Penzance to Kensington milk train approaches the summit between Chasewater and Truro on Saturday, 16 May 1959, hauled by Penzance (83G) based no. 6911 *Holker Hall*. The rear vehicle contains what appears to be a 4-wheeled mobile milk tank. M Mensing

The 1.50pm service from Bristol TM to Paddington passes through the small station at Box on 20 June 1959, hauled by no. 6914 *Langton Hall* (83B). On the right is the site of the small ex-broad gauge engine shed that closed in 1919. The water tank is still in situ.
P A Fry/Great Western Trust

A great night view of no. 4956 *Plowden Hall* from Cardiff Canton (86C) as it waits at Oxford with the evening Grimsby to Swindon fish train in late July 1959. This service was often used by Swindon as an ex-works running in turn. No. 4956 is indeed being run in after a Heavy Intermediate repair at Swindon.
J D Edwards

The 6.08pm Fridays only relief service from Paddington to Birmingham and Wolverhampton speeds through Beaconsfield on 24 July 1959, hauled by no. 4994 *Downton Hall* (81E). B W Leslie/Great Western Trust

A short Class F freight service probably from the West Midlands approaches Culham Station en route to Didcot in the summer of 1959, hauled by no. 5919 *Worsley Hall* (84B). A feature at Culham were the blue enamel running in boards, one of which can just be seen behind the signal box. J D Edwards

An excellent portrait of very clean no. 5916 *Trinity Hall* from Oxley (84B) in the yard at Oxford MPD in August 1959. It had recently left the works at Swindon after a Heavy Intermediate repair. J D Edwards

No. 4993 *Dalton Hall* (81D) is pictured here at Oxford on 15 August 1959 with an up fast service to Paddington. On the left is the rather dilapidated wooden steam depot. Standing outside is no. 4995 *Easton Hall* (81F). J D Edwards

A view of Carmarthen (87G) on 29 August 1959, with no less than five ex-Great Western mixed traffic types in view, from left to right, nos. 4937 *Lanelay Hall* (87G), 6843 *Poulton Grange* (87F), 4958 *Priory Hall* (87G), 6865 *Hopton Grange* (86A), and 4300 class 2-6-0 no. 6306 (87H). M Hale/Great Western Trust

This interesting picture shows Oxley based no. 5919 *Worsley Hall* on a fitted banana freight from Avonmouth Docks to South Wales via Pilning, passing New Passage Halt on the Avonmouth branch on 28 September 1959. On reaching Pilning the *Hall* will run around its train to continue its journey to South Wales. M Mensing

No. 5917 *Westminster Hall* from Worcester (85A) stands inside
the loco shed Oxford in April 1959. Number 022 chalked on the
smokebox indicates that it had recently worked on the Cathedrals
Express service. At this time the shed roof was under repair. On the
left is the stationary washout boiler and on the right one of Oxford
Castles, no. 7008 *Swansea Castle*. J D Edwards

Modified Hall no. 6987 *Shervington Hall* from Wolverhampton (Road) (84A) passes Gresford Halt, north of Wrexham, with the 9.10pm service from Paddington to Birkenhead on 18 April 1960. The *Hall* would quite probably have taken over from a *King* or a *Castle* Class 4-6-0 at Wolverhampton. Gresford Halt closed to passengers on 10 September 1962. M Mensing

An up class F freight from South Wales, hauled by no. 5981 *Frensham Hall* (82C) in ex-works condition, is pictured here at Chipping Sodbury water troughs on 30 April 1960. P A Fry/Great Western Trust

Looking in pristine condition after a heavy general (HG) repair at Swindon, no. 5945 *Leckhampton Hall* stands outside its home shed at Swindon on 1 May 1960.
P H Kelley

The down *Royal Duchy* from Paddington to Penzance, hauled by no. 5969 *Honington Hall* (81D), is seen here approaching Starcross in June 1960. As already mentioned on Summer Saturdays this service was regularly worked by a *Hall, Modified Hall*.
Great Western Trust

An **up** class C express freight from the South West, probably comprising perishables, is seen here hauled by a clean no. 4905 *Barton Hall* (83A) as it skirts the sea wall at Teignmouth on 10 June 1960. These fast perishable trains were a feature of freight traffic from the South West. Great Western Trust

A nice portrait of the now preserved no. 4979 *Wootton Hall* (81F) as it stands in the yard at Reading on 4 September 1960. B Yates/Great Western Trust

Lacock Halt, Wiltshire, was situated on the line from Thingley Junction to Westbury. It is pictured here on 6 November 1960 as no. 6972 *Beningborough Hall* (82A) speeds through with the 10.10am service from Bristol to Weymouth, via Trowbridge and Westbury.
P A Fry/ Great Western Trust

No. 7924 *Thorneycroft Hall* (82D) speeds through Saltford on 2 December 1960 with the 10.30am service from Cardiff to Portsmouth. It is coupled to Collett tender no. 2549. Saltford signal box was opened in 1909 and closed in November 1960. The station was closed to passengers in January 1970.
P A Fry/Great Western Trust

A head on confrontation on the single line Oxford to Princes Risborough branch at Morris Cowley on 12 January 1961, between ex-LMS 8F no. 48134 from Willesden (1A) the 6.50pm Washwood Heath-Morris Cowley, Hall no. 6979 *Helperly Hall* (84C) on the 12.40am parcels service from Greenford to Leamington Spa, (via Thame). Both locos were subsequently repaired and continued in service for a number of years. No. 48134 was withdrawn in January 1966 and no. 6979 in February 1965. Great Western Trust

Looking rather the worse for wear, no. 6902 *Butlers Hall* (82C) stands outside A shop at Swindon in February 1961. It was damaged whilst hauling a York to Swindon service on 11 February 1961, after it collided with the 1.50am Woodford Halse to Mottram freight, which had derailed between Rugby Central and Lutterworth. Unfortunately the driver of the *Hall*, A. Jones was killed and the fireman and guard were seriously injured. The *Hall* was not repaired, being officially withdrawn on 1 May 1961.
Great Western Trust

No. 4941 *Llangedwyn Hall* from Westbury (82D) climbs out of Weymouth on 15 June 1961 with an up class C fitted freight. Regional boundary changes saw Weymouth become part of the Southern Region from February 1958, hence the upper quadrant signals. M Mensing

A long mixed parcels service, hauled by no. 4925 *Eynsham Hall*, winds its way up the incline from Hockley no.1 tunnel and through Birmingham Snow Hill on 12 August 1961. It was allocated at this time to Southall (81C) from where it was withdrawn on 7 August 1962.
L Hanson/Great Western Trust

The 5.35pm fast service from Oxford to Paddington departs from Oxford behind a rather dirty no. 6992 *Arborfield Hall* (85A) on 30 August 1961. The painted smokebox is probably a result of a recent unclassified repair at Worcester. Departing from Worcester at 3.10pm it ran as a semi-fast service to Oxford, and then as a fast non-stop service to London. Departing from Oxford at 5.35pm service it had a 60 minute schedule for the $63\frac{1}{4}$ mile trip to the capital. W Turner

***Halls* formed** the mainstay of both passenger and freight services through Oxford for many years. Here no. 5973 *Rolleston Hall* from Reading (81D) winds its way through Oxford with an up class H mixed freight service from the West Midlands to the London area in March 1962. W Turner

The **5.35pm** service from Hereford to Paddington is seen here at Worcester Shrub Hill on Good Friday, 20 April 1962 hauled by no.4913 *Baglan Hall* (85C). It was withdrawn just five months later in September 1962. M Mensing

An up class H freight from Banbury to Hinksey Yard, Oxford, passes Aynho water troughs, between Banbury and Oxford, on 19 May 1962, hauled by no. 5936 *Oakley Hall* (81D). On 11 May 1941 no. 5936 was damaged by an enemy aircraft at West Kensington whilst working a milk train to Wood Lane Milk depot. There were no casualties but the *Hall* was badly damaged. It was subsequently repaired, and soon put back into service. Great Western Trust

No. 6928 *Underley Hall* (86G) is pictured here under repair in Swindon A shop in June 1962. This Heavy General repair was the last it received. It was withdrawn from Didcot in June 1965. In the background also under repair is no. 6874 *Haughton Grange*. Great Western Trust

In ex-works condition after a Heavy Intermediate repair, no. 5978 *Bodinnick Hall* (82C) passes slowly through Oxford on 31 May 1962 with a northbound fully fitted freight comprising what appear to be PAL vans. During its visit to the works it was fitted with a Hawksworth AK boiler, and a smaller diameter chimney. Steve Boorne

Oxford (81F) based *Modified Hall* no. 7911 *Lady Margaret Hall* speeds through Charwelton on the ex-Great Central main line with the 11.16am through service from Bournemouth West to Newcastle on 23 June 1962. The use of a Western Region locomotive as far as Leicester became a regular feature during the final years of steam traction, especially on Summer Saturdays.
The late Dr Geoff Smith/ courtesy Mrs B Smith

An unidentified stopping service from Fishguard to Carmarthen is seen here at a wet Clarbeston Road on 28 June 1962. It is hauled by (87J) no. 4962 *Ragley Hall.*

The combined 11.05am/12.45pm Saturdays only service from Ilfracombe and Minehead to Wolverhampton Low Level, hauled by no. 4964 *Rodwell Hall* (84A), is seen here approaching Coaley Station, south of Gloucester, on 7 July 1962. The *Hall* is coupled to Hawksworth 4,000 gallon tender no. 4094. M Mensing

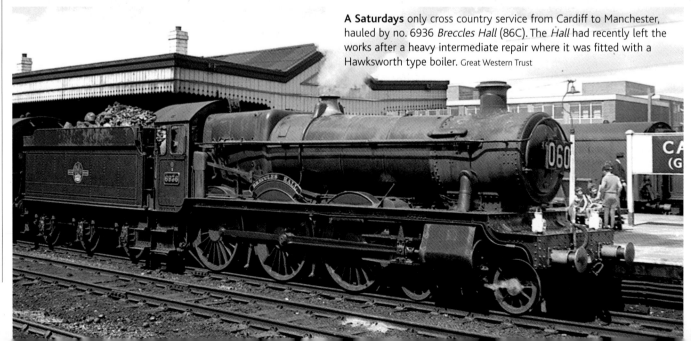

A Saturdays only cross country service from Cardiff to Manchester, hauled by no. 6936 *Breccles Hall* (86C). The *Hall* had recently left the works after a heavy intermediate repair where it was fitted with a Hawksworth type boiler. Great Western Trust

Cardiff Canton based *Halls* were regular performers on the cross country services between Cardiff and Portsmouth Harbour. Pictured here on 4 May 1963 is no. 7925 *Westol Hall* as it departs from Trowbridge on the 10.30am Cardiff, Southampton and Portsmouth service.
M Mensing

No. 5987 *Brocket Hall* (81F) makes a fine sight as it approaches Radley on 8 June 1963 with a down class C freight service for the West Midlands, comprising both perishable and parcels traffic. The nearside track is the branch line from Abingdon, which ran alongside the main line to the junction station at Radley. D Tuck

A down freight hauled by no. 5988 *Bostock Hall* (2A) speeds through Radley, south of Oxford, on 8 October 1963. I have included this picture to show the steel goal post frame that was bolted to the front of some Collett tenders; this held the electrification warning signs and also deterred the crew from climbing onto the tender whilst under the wires. D Tuck

A northbound freight probably to the yard at Woodford Halse is pictured here passing under the vast road bridge near Thorpe Mandeville on the Banbury to Woodford Halse line on 12 October 1963. It is hauled by no. 7901 *Dodington Hall* from Bristol St Phillips Marsh (82B).
M Mensing

A northbound class F fully fitted freight crosses the embankment near Beaconsfield on a sunny 19 December 1963 hauled by Neath (87A) allocated no. 6905 *Claughton Hall.*
G T Robinson/Great Western Trust

Looking in need of a clean and minus nameplates, no. 7917 *North Aston Hall* (81E) is turned at Banbury in readiness for its next duty on 31 January 1965. It had visited Swindon for a light classified repair as late as March 1964. It is a shame that many of these fine locomotives were neglected in their final years. Banbury became part of the London Midland region in 1963, and closed to steam on 3 October 1966. M Soden

The 4.18pm service from Paddington to Banbury was the last steam hauled service over the 'Cut Off' route. The service comprising four coaches and a van is seen here at High Wycombe on 25 February 1965, hauled by a rather rundown no. 6911 (*Holker Hall*). Apart from the number chalked on the smokebox, and a Banbury (2D) shedplate, the locomotive carries no other identification. It was withdrawn just a few weeks later on 11 April 1965. P H Kelley

Didcot closed to steam on 14 July 1965, after which date its *Hall* allocation moved up the line to Oxford. Pictured here on the ash road at Didcot on 9 March 1965 is no. 6921 *Borwick Hall* (81E) minus nameplates. It was withdrawn from Oxford in October 1965. Great Western Trust

With only its smokebox numberplate left as identification, no. 5933 (*Kingsway Hall*) stands at Reading General on 17 June 1965 with a down parcels. It did not see out the year, being withdrawn in August. P H Kelley

A silhouette of no. 5971 *Merevale Hall* (81F) seen here passing Wolvercote, November 1965, the through service between Bournemouth, York and Newcastle. This service which departed from Oxford at 2.10pm was the last regular main line passenger working for an ex-Great Western *Hall* Class on the Western Region. The final run being made between Oxford and Banbury by no. 6998 *Burton Agnes Hall*, on 3 January 1966.
The late Dr G Smith/courtesy Mrs B Smith

APPENDIX

Number	Name	Built	First shed	Last shed	Withdrawn	Final Mlieage	Notes
2925	*Saint Martin*	Sep-07	Newton Abbot	Shrewsbury	Aug-24	778,209	converted to *Hall* 8/24
2925	*Saint Martin*	Dec-24	Laira	Old Oak Common	Apr-59	1,304,291	renumberd 4900 on 7 Dec 1928
4901	*Adderley Hall*	Dec-28	Penzance	Stafford Rd	Sep-60	1,263,627	
4902	*Aldenham Hall*	Dec-28	Penzance	Taunton	Sep-63	1,280,358	
4903	*Astley Hall*	Dec-28	Penzance	Worcester	Oct-64	1,340,597	
4904	*Binnegar Hall*	Dec-28	Penzance	Taunton	Dec-63	1,288,079	
4905	*Barton Hall*	Dec-28	Truro	Didcot	Nov-63	1,370,858	
4906	*Bradfield Hall*	Jan-29	Truro	Oxley	Sep-62	1,341,287	
4907	*Broughton Hall*	Jan-29	Laira	Hereford	Aug-63	1,252,377	renumbered 3903 5/47-4/50
4908	*Broome Hall*	Jan-29	Laira	Didcot	Oct-63	1,408,430	
4909	*Blakesley Hall*	Jan-29	Laira	Swindon	Sep-62	1,321,819	
4910	*Blaisdon Hall*	Jan-29	Laira	Didcot	Dec-63	1,367,749	
4911	*Bowden Hall*	Feb-29	Laira	Truro	Apr-41	558,921	destroyed wartime bomb damage
4912	*Berrington Hall*	Feb-29	Laira	Oxley	Aug-62	1,345,017	
4913	*Baglan Hall*	Feb-29	Laira	Hereford	Sep-62	1,347,386	
4914	*Cranmore Hall*	Feb-29	Laira	St Philips Marsh	Dec-63	1,259,673	
4915	*Condover Hall*	Feb-29	Gloucester	Reading	Feb-63	1,328,672	
4916	*Crumlin Hall*	Feb-29	Gloucester	Swindon	Aug-64	1,287,830	
4917	*Crosswood Hall*	Mar-29	Old Oak Common	Westbury	Sep-62	1,376,381	
4918	*Dartington Hall*	Mar-29	Old Oak Common	Cardiff East Dock	Jun-63	1,309,911	
4919	*Donnington Hall*	Mar-29	Old Oak Common	Worcester	Oct-64	1,320,248	
4920	*Dumbleton Hall*	Mar-29	Old Oak Common	Barrow Rd	Dec-65	1,396,966	Preserved South Devon Rly
4921	*Eaton Hall*	Apr-29	Old Oak Common	Reading	Sep-62	1,273,602	
4922	*Enville Hall*	Apr-29	Old Oak Common	Oxford	Jul-63	1,287,068	
4923	*Evenley Hall*	Apr-29	St. Philips Marsh	Banbury	May-64	1,353,155	
4924	*Eydon Hall*	May-29	Old Oak Common	Swindon	Oct-63	1,364,143	
4925	*Eynsham Hall*	May-29	Old Oak Common	Southall	Aug-62	1,319,376	
4926	*Fairleigh Hall*	May-29	Old Oak Common	Pontypool Rd	Sep-61	1,200,131	
4927	*Farnborough Hall*	May-29	Old Oak Common	Llanelly	Sep-63	1,416,636	
4928	*Gatacre Hall*	May-29	Stafford Rd	Cardiff East Dock	Dec-63	1,339,378	
4929	*Goytrey Hall*	May-29	Stafford Rd	Gloucester	Mar-65	1,397,264	
4930	*Hagley Hall*	May-29	Stafford Rd	Swindon	Dec-63	1,295,236	Preserved Severn Valley Rly
4931	*Hanbury Hall*	May-29	Stafford Rd	Cardiff Canton	Jul-62	1,300,002	
4932	*Hatherton Hall*	Jun-29	Stafford Rd	Severn Tunnel Jct	Nov-64	1,359,393	
4933	*Himley Hall*	Jun-29	Bath Road	Shrewsbury	Aug-64	1,259,049	
4934	*Hindlip Hall*	Jun-29	Bath Road	Taunton	Sep-62	1,213,555	
4935	*Ketley Hall*	Jun-29	Chester	Didcot	Mar-63	1,358,688	
4936	*Kinlet Hall*	Jun-29	Chester	Cardiff East Dock	Jan-64	1,339,061	
4937	*Lanelay Hall*	Jun-29	Stafford Rd	Pontypool Rd	Sep-62	1,306,064	
4938	*Liddington Hall*	Jun-29	Bath Road	Llanelly	Nov-62	1,287,128	
4939	*Littleton Hall*	Jul-29	Truro	Didcot	Feb-63	1,228,917	
4940	*Ludford Hall*	Jul-29	Taunton	Taunton	Nov-59	1,284,530	First *Hall* withdrawn

Number	Name	Built	First shed	Last shed	Withdrawn	Final Mlieage	Notes
4941	Llangedwyn Hall	Jul-29	Newton Abbot	Westbury	Sep-62	1,242,665	
4942	Maindy Hall	Jul-29	Newton Abbot	Didcot	Dec-63	1,259,332	Preserved Didcot Saint project
4943	Marrington Hall	Jul-29	Old Oak Common	Pontypool Rd	Dec-63	1,353,901	
4944	Middleton Hall	Jul-29	Old Oak Common	Southall	Sep-62	1,257,046	
4945	Milligan Hall	Aug-29	Basingstoke	Southall	Nov-61	1,318,692	
4946	Moseley Hall	Aug-29	Bath Road	Shrewsbury	Jun-63	1,240,751	
4947	Nanhoran Hall	Aug-29	Gloucester	St Philips Marsh	Sep-62	1,352,851	
4948	Northwick Hall	Aug-29	Bath Road	Swindon	Sep-62	1,293,341	renumbered 3902 5/47-9/48
4949	Packwood Hall	Aug-29	Stafford Rd	Barrow Rd	Sep-64	1,355,415	
4950	Patshull Hall	Aug-29	Stafford Rd	Didcot	May-64	1,310,762	
4951	Pendeford Hall	Jul-29	Old Oak Common	Oxford	Jun-64	1,334,554	
4952	Peplow Hall	Aug-29	Bath Road	Cardiff Canton	Sep-62	1,270,461	
4953	Pitchford Hall	Aug-29	Bath Road	Cardiff East Dock	May-63	1,344,464	Preserved Epping & Ongar Rly
4954	Plaish Hall	Aug-29	Stafford Rd	Oxley	Nov-64	1,341,161	
4955	Plaspower Hall	Aug-29	Bath Road	Pontypool Rd	Nov-63	1,320,257	
4956	Plowden Hall	Sep-29	Old Oak Common	Westbury	Jul-63	1,343,127	
4957	Postlip Hall	Sep-29	Old Oak Common	Reading	Apr-62	1,288,249	
4958	Priory Hall	Sep-29	Oxley	Gloucester	Sep-64	1,316,540	
4959	Purley Hall	Sep-29	Westbury	Didcot	Dec-64	1,278,546	
4960	Pyle Hall	Sep-29	Westbury	St Philips Marsh	Sep-62	1,282,859	
4961	Pyrland Hall	Nov-29	Goodwick	Reading	Oct-62	1,350,042	
4962	Ragley Hall	Nov-29	Cardiff Canton	Oxford	Oct-65	1,405,224	
4963	Rignall Hall	Nov-29	Carmarthen	Worcester	Jun-62	1,230,706	
4964	Rodwell Hall	Nov-29	Goodwick	Pontypool Rd	Oct-63	1,229,929	
4965	Rood Ashton Hall	Nov-29	Oxley	Didcot	Apr-62	1,168,515	Preserved Tyseley Works
4966	Shakenhurst Hall	Nov-29	Basingstoke	Oxford	Nov-63	1,329,611	
4967	Shirenewton Hall	Dec-29	Tyseley	Neath	Sep-62	1,274,429	
4968	Shotton Hall	Dec-29	Old Oak Common	St. Philips Marsh	Jul-62	1,205,525	Renumbered 3900 5/47-3/49
4969	Shrugborough Hall	Dec-29	Old Oak Common	Southall	Sep-62	1,214,340	
4970	Sketty Hall	Dec-29	Old Oak Common	Duffryn Yard	Jul-63	1,344,048	
4971	Stanway Hall	Jan-30	Old Oak Common	Cardiff Canton	Aug-62	1,281,229	Renumbered 3901 5/47-4/49
4972	Saint Brides Hall	Jan-30	Old Oak Common	Westbury	Feb-64	1,315,534	Renumbered 3904 5/47-10/48
4973	Sweeney Hall	Jan-30	Penzance	Cardiff Canton	Jul-62	1,314,618	
4974	Talgarth Hall	Jan-30	Penzance	Gloucester	Apr-62	1,273,651	
4975	Umberslade Hall	Jan-30	Penzance	Oxford	Sep-63	1,298,925	
4976	Warfield Hall	Jan-30	Penzance	Oxford	May-64	1,280,182	
4977	Watcombe Hall	Jan-30	Penzance	Cardiff Canton	May-62	1,260,721	
4978	Westwood Hall	Feb-30	Laira	Severn Tunnel Jct	Sep-64	1,331,101	
4979	Wootton Hall	Feb-30	Laira	Oxford	Dec-63	1,233,801	Preserved Ribble Railway Preston
4980	Wrottesley Hall	Feb-30	Penzance	St Philips Marsh	Jul-63	1,213,359	
4981	Abberley Hall	Dec-30	Oxley	Oxford	Oct-63	1,274,585	
4982	Acton Hall	Jan-31	Weymouth	Goodwick	May-62	1,245,012	
4983	Albert Hall	Jan-31	Cardiff Canton	St Philips Marsh	Dec-63	1,199,562	
4984	Albrighton Hall	Jan-31	Worcester	Cardiff Canton	Sep-62	1,231,044	
4985	Allesley Hall	Jan-31	Old Oak Common	Neath	Sep-64	1,253,139	
4986	Aston Hall	Jan-31	Penzance	Southall	May-62	1,222,109	
4987	Brockley Hall	Jan-31	Carmarthen	Southall	Apr-62	1,195,979	
4988	Bulwell Hall	Jan-31	Old Oak Common	Oxford	Feb-64	1,205,459	
4989	Cherwell Hall	Feb-31	Penzance	Severn Tunnel Jct	Nov-64	1,216,039	
4990	Clifton Hall	Feb-31	Penzance	Hereford	Apr-62	1,150,964	
4991	Cobham Hall	Feb-31	St Philips Marsh	Swindon	Dec-63	1,270,339	

Number	Name	Built	First shed	Last shed	Withdrawn	Final Mlieage	Notes
4992	*Crosby Hall*	Feb-31	Penzance	Barrow Rd	Sep-62	1,268,293	
4993	*Dalton Hall*	Feb-31	Penzance	Severn Tunnel Jct	Feb-65	1,192,446	
4994	*Downton Hall*	Feb-31	Penzance	Didcot	Mar-63	1,143,348	
4995	*Easton Hall*	Feb-31	Laira	Southall	Jun-62	1,217,636	
4996	*Eden Hall*	Jan-31	Old Oak Common	Taunton	Sep-63	1,185,556	
4997	*Elton Hall*	Mar-31	Oxford	Oxley	Oct-61	1,148,456	
4998	*Eyton Hall*	Mar-31	Old Oak Common	Banbury	Oct-63	1,254,441	
4999	*Gopsal Hall*	Mar-31	Old Oak Common	St Philips Marsh	Sep-62	1,262,589	
5900	*Hinderton Hall*	Mar-31	Old Oak Common	St Philips Marsh	Dec-63	1,200,282	Preserved Didcot Railway Centre
5901	*Hazel Hall*	May-31	Truro	Reading	Jun-64	1,159,566	
5902	*Howick Hall*	May-31	Truro	St Philips Marsh	Nov-62	1,211,388	
5903	*Keele Hall*	May-31	Stafford Rd	Llanelly	Sep-63	1,232,460	
5904	*Kelham Hall*	May-31	Old Oak Common	St Philips Marsh	Nov-63	1,261,250	
5905	*Knowsley Hall*	May-31	Swindon	Goodwick	Jul-63	1,262,580	
5906	*Lawton Hall*	May-31	St Philips Marsh	Reading	May-62	1,124,590	
5907	*Marble Hall*	May-31	Newton Abbot	Reading	Nov-61	1,148,244	
5908	*Moreton Hall*	Jun-31	Swindon	St Philips Marsh	Jul-63	1,273,198	
5909	*Newton Hall*	Jun-31	St Philips Marsh	Cardiff Canton	Jul-62	1,187,420	
5910	*Park Hall*	Jun-31	Old Oak Common	Oxley	Sep-62	1,295,056	
5911	*Preston Hall*	Jun-31	Carmarthen	Cardiff Canton	Sep-62	1,239,075	
5912	*Queen's Hall*	Jun-31	Oxford	Banbury	Dec-62	1,168,321	
5913	*Rushton Hall*	Jun-31	Landore	Exeter	May-62	1,177,288	
5914	*Ripon Hall*	Jul-31	Old Oak Common	Gloucester	Jan-64	1,209,922	
5915	*Trentham Hall*	Jul-31	Banbury	Reading	Jan-60	1,126,453	
5916	*Trinity Hall*	Jul-31	Shrewsbury	Oxley	Jul-62	1,200,731	
5917	*Westminster Hall*	Jul-31	Bath Road	Southall	Sep-62	1,198,707	
5918	*Walton Hall*	Jul-31	Bath Road	Oxford	Sep-62	1,123,847	
5919	*Worsley Hall*	Jul-31	Bath Road	Old Oak Common	Aug-63	1,188,085	
5920	*Wyecliff Hall*	Aug-31	Leamington	Westbury	Jan-62	1,181,312	
5921	*Bingley Hall*	May-33	Reading	Westbury	Jan-62	1,121,884	
5922	*Caxton Hall*	May-33	Old Oak Common	Oxford	Jan-64	1,203,947	
5923	*Colston Hall*	May-33	Old Oak Common	Oxford	Dec-63	1,211,759	
5924	*Dinton Hall*	May-33	Reading	St Philips Marsh	Dec-63	1,161,143	
5925	*Eastcote Hall*	May-33	Old Oak Common	Westbury	Oct-62	1,205,975	
5926	*Grotrian Hall*	Jun-33	Old Oak Common	Banbury	Sep-62	1,263,834	
5927	*Guild Hall*	Jun-33	Old Oak Common	Tyseley	Oct-64	1,180,726	
5928	*Haddon Hall*	Jun-33	Goodwick	Goodwick	May-62	1,030,390	Goodwick all of its working life
5929	*Hanham Hall*	Jun-33	St Philips Marsh	Pontypool Rd	Nov-63	1,096,640	
5930	*Hannington Hall*	Jun-33	Oxley	Worcester	Sep-62	1,037,428	
5931	*Hatherley Hall*	Jun-33	Old Oak Common	Old Oak Common	Sep-62	1,239,444	
5932	*Haydon Hall*	Jun-33	Bath Road	Barrow Rd	Oct-65	1,284,369	
5933	*Kingsway Hall*	Jun-33	Bath Road	Oxford	Aug-65	1,131,460	
5934	*Kneller Hall*	Jun-33	Stafford Rd	St Philips Marsh	May-64	1,223,568	
5935	*Norton Hall*	Jul-33	Stafford Rd	Cardiff Canton	May-62	1,097,229	
5936	*Oakley Hall*	Jul-33	Old Oak Common	Gloucester	Jan-65	1,294,179	
5937	*Stanford Hall*	Jul-33	Penzance	Cardiff East Dock	Nov-63	1,329,929	
5938	*Stanley Hall*	Jul-33	Stafford Rd	Newport Ebbw Jct	May-63	1,239,861	
5939	*Tangley Hall*	Jul-33	Laira	Newport Ebbw Jct	Oct-64	1,260,470	
5940	*Whitbourne Hall*	Aug-33	Stafford Rd	St Philips Marsh	Sep-62	1,265,086	
5941	*Campion Hall*	Feb-35	Old Oak Common	St Philips Marsh	Jul-62	1,112,729	
5942	*Doldowlod Hall*	Feb-35	Old Oak Common	Tyseley	Dec-63	1,045,711	

Number	Name	Built	First shed	Last shed	Withdrawn	Final Mlieage	Notes
5943	Elmdon Hall	Mar-35	Westbury	Swindon	Jun-63	1,079,012	
5944	Ickenham Hall	Mar-35	Oxley	Gloucester	Apr-63	1,043,644	
5945	Leckhampton Hall	Mar-35	Oxley	Oxford	Apr-63	1,117,981	
5946	Marwell Hall	Mar-35	Cardiff Canton	Goodwick	Jul-62	1,138,917	
5947	Saint Benet's Hall	Mar-35	Oxley	Banbury	Jul-62	1,042,881	
5948	Siddington Hall	Mar-35	Didcot	Pontypool Rd	Aug-63	1,051,218	
5949	Trematon Hall	Apr-35	Weymouth	Swindon	May-61	1,074,921	
5950	Wardley Hall	Apr-35	Old Oak Common	Westbury	Nov-61	1,032,140	
5951	Clyffe Hall	Dec-35	Gloucester	Gloucester	Apr-64	1,029,270	Gloucester loco all its life
5952	Cogan Hall	Dec-35	Penzance	Hereford	Jun-64	1,074,911	parts used for Betton Grange project
5953	Dunley Hall	Dec-35	Penzance	St Philips Marsh	Oct-62	1,044,827	
5954	Faendre Hall	Dec-35	Old Oak Common	St Philips Marsh	Oct-63	1,014,761	
5955	Garth Hall	Dec-35	Stafford Rd	Barrow Rd	Apr-65	1,037,300	renumbered 3950 6/46-10/48
5956	Horsley Hall	Dec-35	Worcester	Oxford	Mar-63	979,776	
5957	Hutton Hall	Dec-35	Oxley	Oxford	Jul-64	1,000,374	
5958	Knolton Hall	Jan-36	Taunton	St Philips Marsh	Mar-64	1,116,653	
5959	Mawley Hall	Jan-36	Reading	Tyseley	Sep-62	1,069,787	
5960	Saint Edmund Hall	Jan-36	Oxford	Oxford	Sep-62	1,037,156	
5961	Toynbee Hall	Jun-36	Stafford Rd	Neath	Aug-65	996,957	
5962	Wantage Hall	Jul-36	Old Oak Common	Worcester	Nov-64	1,042,054	
5963	Wimpole Hall	Jul-36	Landore	St Philips Marsh	Jun-64	1,140,896	
5964	Wolseley Hall	Jul-36	Swindon	Westbury	Sep-62	1,013,256	
5965	Woollas Hall	Aug-36	Hereford	Tyseley	Jul-62	1,019,611	
5966	Ashford Hall	Mar-37	Oxley	Oxford	Sep-62	893,114	
5967	Bickmarsh Hall	Mar-37	Chester	Westbury	Jun-64	1,005,067	Preserved Northampton & Lamport
5968	Cory Hall	Mar-37	Westbury	Gloucester	Sep-62	908,492	
5969	Honington Hall	Apr-37	Bath Road	Carmarthen	Sep-62	1,019,388	
5970	Hengrave Hall	Apr-37	Cardiff Canton	Hereford	Oct-63	1,043,315	
5971	Merevale Hall	Apr-37	Weymouth	Oxford	Dec-65	956,920	
5972	Olton Hall	Apr-37	Neath	Cardiff East Dock	Dec-63	1,013,325	Preserved West Coast Rly
5973	Rolleston Hall	May-37	Old Oak Common	Reading	Sep-62	888,710	
5974	Wallsworth Hall	Apr-37	Westbury	Severn Tunnel Jct	Dec-64	1,070,686	
5975	Winslow Hall	May-37	Westbury	Barrow Rd	Jul-64	1,088,921	
5976	Ashwicke Hall	Sep-38	Tyseley	Pontypool Rd	Jul-64	911,848	Renumbered 3951 4/47-11/48
5977	Beckford Hall	Sep-38	Worcester	Oxford	Aug-63	919,369	
5978	Bodinnick Hall	Sep-38	Old Oak Common	St Philips Marsh	Oct-63	945,406	
5979	Cruckton Hall	Sep-38	Bath Road	Worcester	Nov-64	893,201	
5980	Dingley Hall	Sep-38	Gloucester	Gloucester	Sep-62	873,786	
5981	Frensham Hall	Oct-38	Stafford Rd	Neath	Sep-62	808,362	
5982	Harrington Hall	Oct-38	Carmarthen	Reading	Aug-62	891,615	
5983	Henley Hall	Oct-38	Worcester	Tyseley	Apr-65	922,140	
5984	Linden Hall	Oct-38	Weymouth	Cardiff East Dock	Jan-65	917,443	
5985	Mostyn Hall	Oct-38	Old Oak Common	Oxford	Sep-63	924,251	
5986	Arbury Hall	Nov-39	Reading	Westbury	Sep-63	796,306	Renumbered 3954 5/47-2/50
5987	Brocket Hall	Nov-39	Old Oak Common	Oxford	Jan-64	937,021	
5988	Bostock Hall	Nov-39	Hereford	Tyseley	Oct-65	782,729	
5989	Cransley Hall	Dec-39	Oxley	Neath	Jul-62	741,594	
5990	Dorford Hall	Dec-39	Gloucester	Banbury	Jan-65	867,836	
5991	Gresham Hall	Dec-39	Banbury	Shrewsbury	Jul-64	803,940	
5992	Horton Hall	Dec-39	Banbury	Newport Ebbw Jct	Sep-65	864,867	
5993	Kirby Hall	Dec-39	Tyseley	Reading	May-63	854,055	

Number	Name	Built	First shed	Last shed	Withdrawn	Final Mlieage	Notes
5994	*Roydon Hall*	Dec-39	Shrewsbury	Shrewsbury	Mar-63	802,918	
5995	*Wick Hall*	Jan-40	Stafford Rd	Oxley	Apr-63	835,560	
5996	*Mytton Hall*	Jun-40	Old Oak Common	Oxley	Sep-62	865,093	
5997	*Sparkford Hall*	Jun-40	Tyseley	Swindon	Jul-62	842,719	
5998	*Trevor Hall*	Jun-40	Laira	Pontypool Rd	Mar-64	927,489	
5999	*Wollaton Hall*	Jun-40	Newton Abbot	Westbury	Sep-62	838,329	
6900	*Abney Hall*	Jul-40	Old Oak Common	Barrow Rd	Oct-64	899,413	
6901	*Arley Hall*	Jul-40	Stafford Rd	Pontypool Rd	Jun-64	844,703	
6902	*Butlers Hall*	Jul-40	Old Oak Common	Swindon	May-61	788,144	
6903	*Belmont Hall*	Jul-40	Landore	Banbury	Sep-65	832,108	
6904	*Charfield Hall*	Jul-40	Banbury	Banbury	Jan-65	868,186	
6905	*Claughton Hall*	Jul-40	Worcester	Neath	Jun-64	836,842	
6906	*Chicheley Hall*	Nov-40	Banbury	Banbury	Apr-65	752,116	
6907	*Davenham Hall*	Nov-40	Newton Abbot	Banbury	Feb-65	865,955	
6908	*Downham Hall*	Nov-40	Stafford Rd	Barrow Rd	Jul-65	825,391	
6909	*Frewin Hall*	Nov-40	Old Oak Common	Didcot	Jun-64	863,104	
6910	*Gossington Hall*	Dec-40	Old Oak Common	Oxford	Oct-65	836,776	
6911	*Holker Hall*	Jan-41	Newton Abbot	Banbury	Apr-65	917,367	
6912	*Helmster Hall*	Jan-41	St Philips Marsh	Cardiff East Dock	Feb-64	842,182	
6913	*Levens Hall*	Feb-41	Laira	Gloucester	Jun-64	901,037	
6914	*Langton Hall*	Feb-41	Tyseley	Cardiff East Dock	Apr-64	845,804	
6915	*Mursley Hall*	Feb-41	Stafford Rd	Banbury	Feb-65	855,695	
6916	*Misterton Hall*	Jun-41	St Philips Marsh	Banbury	Aug-65	824,084	
6917	*Oldlands Hall*	Jun-41	Gloucester	Banbury	Sep-65	832,604	
6918	*Sandon Hall*	Jun-41	Landore	Barrow Rd	Sep-65	807,484	
6919	*Tylney Hall*	Jun-41	Carmarthen	St. Philips Marsh	Aug-63	853,336	
6920	*Barningham Hall*	Jul-41	Old Oak Common	Duffryn Yard	Nov-63	867,477	
6921	*Borwick Hall*	Jul-41	Hereford	Oxford	Oct-65	846,637	
6922	*Burton Hall*	Jul-41	St Philips Marsh	Tyseley	Apr-65	815,465	
6923	*Croxteth Hall*	Jul-41	Didcot	Oxford	Dec-65	735,168	
6924	*Grantley Hall*	Aug-41	Stafford Rd	Oxford	Oct-65	774,155	
6925	*Hackness Hall*	Aug-41	Old Oak Common	Oxley	Nov-64	772,528	
6926	*Holkham Hall*	Nov-41	Newport Ebbw Jct	Banbury	May-65	725,393	
6927	*Lilford Hall*	Nov-41	Newport Ebbw Jct	Oxford	Oct-65	816,878	
6928	*Underley Hall*	Nov-41	Cardiff Canton	Didcot	Jun-65	848,570	
6929	*Whorlton Hall*	Nov-41	Banbury	Banbury	Oct-63	716,550	
6930	*Aldersey Hall*	Nov-41	Worcester	Banbury	Oct-65	779,061	
6931	*Aldborough Hall*	Dec-41	Truro	Oxford	Oct-65	809,490	
6932	*Burwarton Hall*	Dec-41	Oxley	Oxford	Dec-65	811,166	
6933	*Birtles Hall*	Dec-41	Oxford	Oxley	Nov-64	805,814	
6934	*Beachamwell Hall*	Dec-41	Newton Abbot	Banbury	Oct-65	711,344	
6935	*Browsholme Hall*	Dec-41	Hereford	Cardiff East Dock	Feb-65	845,422	
6936	*Breccles Hall*	Jul-42	Worcester	Cardiff East Dock	Nov-64	800,505	
6937	*Conyngham Hall*	Jul-42	Oxford	Didcot	Dec-65	752,864	
6938	*Corndean Hall*	Jul-42	Worcester	Didcot	Mar-65	840,518	
6939	*Calveley Hall*	Jun-42	Oxley	Cardiff East Dock	Nov-63	798,728	
6940	*Didlington Hall*	Aug-42	Gloucester	Gloucester	May-64	776,650	
6941	*Fillongley Hall*	Aug-42	Chester	Pontypool Rd	Apr-64	758,387	
6942	*Eshton Hall*	Aug-42	Oxley	Gloucester	Dec-64	713,905	
6943	*Farnley Hall*	Aug-42	Worcester	Gloucester	Dec-63	805,225	
6944	*Fledborough Hall*	Sep-42	St Philips Marsh	Severn Tunnel Jct	Nov-65	819,110	

Number	Name	Built	First shed	Last shed	Withdrawn	Final Mlieage	Notes
6945	*Glasfryn Hall*	Sep-42	St Philips Marsh	Cardiff East Dock	Sep-64	778,560	
6946	*Heatherton Hall*	Dec-42	Cardiff Canton	Pontypool Rd	Jun-64	779,808	
6947	*Helmingham Hall*	Dec-42	Worcester	Oxford	Nov-65	763,192	
6948	*Holbrooke Hall*	Dec-42	Cardiff Canton	Worcester	Dec-63	820,876	
6949	*Haberfield Hall*	Dec-42	Landore	Shrewsbury	May-61	687,396	Renumbered 3955 5/47-4/49
6950	*Kingsthorpe Hall*	Dec-42	Worcester	Cardiff East Dock	Jun-64	769,964	
6951	*Impney Hall*	Feb-43	Worcester	Tyseley	Dec-65	780,416	
6952	*Kimberley Hall*	Feb-43	Didcot	Tyseley	Dec-65	686,211	
6953	*Leighton Hall*	Feb-43	Reading	Oxford	Dec-65	737,316	Renumbered 3953 4/47-9/48
6954	*Lotherton Hall*	Mar-43	St Philips Marsh	St Philips Marsh	May-64	781,928	St Phillips Marsh all its working life
6955	*Lydcott Hall*	Mar-43	St Philips Marsh	Severn Tunnel Jct	Feb-65	768,411	
6956	*Mottram Hall*	Mar-43	Oxley	Oxford	Dec-65	747,189	
6957	*Norcliffe Hall*	Apr-43	Newton Abbot	Oxford	Mar-65	733,784	Renumbered 3952 4/47-3/50
6958	*Oxburgh Hall*	Apr-43	Bath Road	Worcester	Jun-65	791,485	
6959	*Peatling Hall*	Mar-44	Swindon	Oxford	Dec-65	814,475	
6960	*Raveningham Hall*	Mar-44	Old Oak Common	Oxford	Jun-64	751,757	Preserved West Somerset Rly
6961	*Stedham Hall*	Mar-44	Westbury	Oxford	Sep-65	801,302	
6962	*Soughton Hall*	Apr-44	Bath Road	Old Oak Common	Jan-63	780,720	
6963	*Throwley Hall*	Apr-44	Stafford Rd	Oxford	Dec-65	692,647	
6964	*Thornbridge Hall*	May-44	Stafford Rd	Banbury	Sep-65	710,592	
6965	*Thirlestaine Hall*	Jul-44	Gloucester	Barrow Rd	Oct-65	728,794	
6966	*Witchingham Hall*	May-44	Swindon	Oxford	Sep-64	751,648	
6967	*Willesley Hall*	Aug-44	Oxley	Oxford	Dec-65	711,328	
6968	*Woodcock Hall*	Sep-44	Old Oak Common	Westbury	Sep-63	761,414	
6969	*Wraysbury Hall*	Apr-44	Severn Tunnel Jct	Didcot	Feb-65	732,440	
6970	*Whaddon Hall*	Sep-44	Oxley	Oxford	Jun-64	726,042	
6971	*Athelhampton Hall*	Oct-44	Bath Road	Tyseley	Oct-64	692,377	
6972	*Beningbrough Hall*	Oct-47	Bath Road	St Philips Marsh	Mar-64	669,791	
6973	*Bricklehampton Hall*	Oct-47	Old Oak Common	Barrow Rd	Aug-65	709,714	
6974	*Bryngwyn Hall*	Oct-47	Old Oak Common	Oxford	May-65	683,108	
6975	*Capesthorpe Hall*	Oct-47	Oxley	Neath	Dec-63	575,906	
6976	*Graythwaite Hall*	Oct-47	Shrewsbury	Banbury	Oct-65	588,803	
6977	*Grundisburgh Hall*	Nov-47	Old Oak Common	Westbury	Dec-63	641,911	
6978	*Haroldstone Hall*	Nov-47	Salisbury	Newport Ebbw Jct	Jul-65	667,304	
6979	*Helperly Hall*	Nov-47	Banbury	Banbury	Feb-65	551,309	
6980	*Llanrumney Hall*	Nov-47	Shrewsbury	Banbury	Oct-65	600,589	
6981	*Marbury Hall*	Feb-48	Weston-super-Mare	St Philips Marsh	Mar-64	624,801	
6982	*Melmerby Hall*	Jan-48	Westbury	Barrow Rd	Aug-64	661,781	
6983	*Otterington Hall*	Feb-48	Old Oak Common	Oxford	Aug-65	599,364	
6984	*Owsden Hall*	Feb-48	Hereford	Barrow Rd	Dec-65	594,835	Preserved Swindon & Cricklade Rly
6985	*Parwick Hall*	Feb-48	Oxley	Gloucester	Sep-64	628,809	
6986	*Rydal Hall*	Mar-48	Tyseley	Didcot	Apr-65	584,585	
6987	*Shervington Hall*	Mar-48	Gloucester	Cardiff East Dock	Sep-64	560,811	
6988	*Swithland Hall*	Mar-48	Weymouth	Westbury	Sep-64	716,590	
6989	*Wightwick Hall*	Mar-48	Hereford	Gloucester	Jun-64	640,645	Preserved Buckingham Railway Centre
6990	*Witherslack Hall*	Apr-48	Old Oak Common	Barrow Rd	Dec-65	632,007	Preserved Great Central Rly
6991	*Acton Burnell Hall*	Nov-48	Westbury	Oxford	Dec-65	582,713	
6992	*Arborfield Hall*	Nov-48	Gloucester	Worcester	Jun-64	557,796	
6993	*Arthog Hall*	Dec-48	Weymouth	Oxford	Dec-65	561,455	
6994	*Baggrave Hall*	Dec-48	Exeter	Oxley	Nov-64	695,284	
6995	*Benthall Hall*	Dec-48	Taunton	Worcester	Mar-65	620,435	

Number	Name	Built	First shed	Last shed	Withdrawn	Final Mlieage	Notes
6996	*Blackwell Hall*	Jan-49	Reading	Didcot	Oct-64	596,389	
6997	*Bryn-Ivor Hall*	Jan-49	Cardiff Canton	Barrow Rd	Nov-64	599,217	
6998	*Burton Agnes Hall*	Jan-49	Cardiff Canton	Oxford	Dec-65	554,089	Preserved Didcot Railway Centre
6999	*Capel Dewi Hall*	Feb-49	Cardiff Canton	Oxford	Dec-65	596,844	
7900	*St. Peter's Hall*	Apr-49	Swindon	Oxford	Dec-64	536,831	
7901	*Dodington Hall*	Mar-49	Bath Road	St. Philips Marsh	Feb-64	633,763	
7902	*Eaton Mascot Hall*	Mar-49	Old Oak Common	Old Oak Common	Jun-64	582,372	Old Oak Common all of its working life
7903	*Foremarke Hall*	Apr-49	Old Oak Common	Cardiff East Dock	Jun-64	621,101	Preserved Glouc and Warwick Railway
7904	*Fountains Hall*	Apr-49	Old Oak Common	Oxford	Dec-65	623,718	
7905	*Fowey Hall*	Apr-49	Laira	Banbury	May-64	545,605	
7906	*Fron Hall*	Dec-49	St Philips Marsh	Oxford	Mar-65	502,924	
7907	*Hart Hall*	Jan-50	St Philips Marsh	Oxford	Dec-65	544,423	
7908	*Henshall Hall*	Jan-50	St Philips Marsh	Tyseley	Oct-65	527,729	
7909	*Haveningham Hall*	Jan-50	Laira	Oxford	Nov-65	577,104	
7910	*Hown Hall*	Jan-50	Southall	Oxford	Feb-65	494,010	
7911	*Lady Margaret Hall*	Feb-50	Old Oak Common	Oxford	Dec-63	500,651	
7912	*Little Linford Hall*	Mar-50	Stafford Rd	Banbury	Oct-65	573,804	
7913	*Little Wyrley Hall*	Mar-50	Tyseley	Severn Tunnel Jct	Mar-65	528,695	
7914	*Lleweni Hall*	Mar-50	Swindon	Barrow Rd	Dec-65	482,992	
7915	*Mere Hall*	Mar-50	Stafford Rd	Tyseley	Oct-65	491,643	
7916	*Mobberley Hall*	Apr-50	St Blazey	Cardiff East Dock	Dec-64	547,672	
7917	*North Aston Hall*	Apr-50	Bath Road	Oxford	Aug-65	618,190	
7918	*Rhose Wood Hall*	Apr-50	Tyseley	Tyseley	Feb-65	533,277	
7919	*Runter Hall*	May-50	Reading	Oxford	Dec-65	487,404	
7920	*Coney Hall*	Sep-50	Gloucester	Worcester	Jun-65	514,474	
7921	*Edstone Hall*	Sep-50	Chester	Old Oak Common	Dec-63	482,155	
7922	*Salford Hall*	Sep-50	Chester	Oxford	Dec-65	463,534	
7923	*Speke Hall*	Sep-50	Swindon	Cardiff East Dock	Jun-65	532,153	
7924	*Thornycroft Hall*	Sep-50	Westbury	Oxford	Dec-65	626,750	
7925	*Westol Hall*	Oct-50	Penzance	Oxford	Dec-65	604,785	
7926	*Willey Hall*	Oct-50	Gloucester	Gloucester	Dec-64	517,205	
7927	*Willington Hall*	Oct-50	Reading	Oxford	Dec-65	456,347	parts used for 'County' project
7928	*Wolf Hall*	Oct-50	Worcester	Worcester	Mar-65	515,812	Worcester all of its working life
7929	*Wyke Hall*	Nov-50	Tyseley	Tyseley	Aug-65	512,080	